I Am a Cat
(II)

I Am a Cat

(II)

SŌSEKI NATSUME

I Am a Cat

(II)

translated by

Aiko Itō and Graeme Wilson

CHARLES E. TUTTLE CO.

Rutland/Vermont : Tokyo/Japan

Chapter 1 originally published in Japan by the
Asahi Shimbun Publishing Company in the *Japan
Quarterly,* Vol. XXI, No. 4.

Published by the Charles E. Tuttle Company, Inc.
of Rutland, Vermont & Tokyo, Japan
with editorial offices at
Suido 1-chome, 2–6, Bunkyo-ku, Tokyo

Library of Congress Catalog Card No. 78–182064
International Standard Book No. 0–8048 1280–2

First printing, 1979
Fifth printing, 1988

PRINTED IN JAPAN

Introduction

THIS INTRODUCTION will be short, essentially because we have little to add to those comments on Natsume Sōseki, his life and work, which were previously offered in the context of our two earlier translations of his writing: *I Am a Cat* (containing the first three chapters of that comic masterpiece) which Charles Tuttle published in 1972, and *Ten Nights of Dream* (containing three of Sōseki's early novellas) from the same publisher in 1974. In the hope that any readers seeking more detailed information about Sōseki may be prepared to consult the Introductions to those two books, this present text will provide only the briefest account of the man and his work, supplemented by a few additional comments specifically relevant to the four chapters of *I Am a Cat* which, printed here together, compose the second volume of an eventual three-volume translation of the complete work.

Natsume Sōseki (1867–1916) was born in Tokyo, the youngest child of a family of minor town-gentry impoverished at the time of the Meiji Restoration of 1868 by loss of his father's hereditary occupation under the Tokugawa shogunate. Extensively educated in both Chinese and Japanese, in 1901 Sōseki was sent to London University (that "godless institution in Gower Street") on a two-year government scholarship which involved a subsequent requirement to teach English literature at Tokyo University (1903–1907). Sōseki so disliked university work that, despite the high social status he thereby forfeited, he took the first possible opportunity to abandon an extremely promising academic career and instead became the literary editor of a major daily newspaper, the *Asahi Shimbun,* in the pages of which he serialized some thirteen novels before his death in 1916. Despite the lateness of his development as a novelist (he was only just short of forty when his first book was published), Sōseki rapidly achieved and has since maintained widespread recognition as the best of modern Japanese novelists. His literary reputation reflects not only the variety, quality and modernity of his novels but the high regard still paid to his works of scholarly criticism, to his enchanting essays and, especially, to his poetry. His *haiku,* strongly influenced by his personal friend Masaoka Shiki, were once considered outstanding but, though they continue to be included in anthologies of modern *haiku,* their diminutive form was not the natural mode for the expression of his genius. His poems in English, poor imitations of the poorest style of Edwardian poetry, are appalling. But his many excellent poems in Chinese, some even written in the month before his death, are the last (or, rather, the most recent) flowering of a formidable tradition of such writing by Japanese poets which, unbroken, extends right back to the *Kaifūsō* of 751.

I Am a Cat, his first novel, began as a single short story (now the first chapter of the total work) commissioned by a literary magazine in 1904 and published in its pages in January 1905. That tale's immediate success resulted in the publication of ten further chapters before, having exhausted the possibilities of his initial idea, Sōseki ended his now extremely long novel by getting his cat intoxicated and so drowning it in a water-butt in October 1906. Partly by reason of the origin of the novel and partly because Sōseki was an admirer and conscious developer of Sterne's picaresque techniques as exemplified in *Tristram Shandy,* almost any chapter of *I Am a Cat* can be read as an independent unit. The book is quintessentially episodic, and it is indeed in direct imitation of Sōseki's own practice (he published successive groups of chapters as three separate books in 1905, 1906 and

1907) that our translation is being published in separate successive volumes. The first single-volume edition of *I Am a Cat* did not, in fact, appear until 1911.

Clearly, the mere length of combined chapters was the major factor in deciding Sōseki upon the points at which to divide *I Am a Cat* into its original three volumes. However, there is a further factor creating a natural break at the end of the third chapter. Much of the charm of the first three chapters resides in their diverting presentation of a cat's view of mankind. The satire is of man in general but the associated case for the superiority of cats, however entertainingly and persuasively put, is not inexhaustible; so that the unique cat-ness of the opening chapters simply could not be maintained in its original and beguiling purity throughout the further chapters demanded by a happily insulted public. Sōseki himself was clearly alive to these considerations, for as early as the opening paragraph of the third chapter the cat apologizes to readers for his growing resemblance to a human being and for his consequent new tendency to criticize humanity as though he, too, were human. Thus the satire in this present book is less specifically feline. In yet later chapters the cat's viewpoint becomes almost totally human, while the object of satire narrows from mankind in general (albeit as exemplified in Meiji middle-class society) to a concentrated satirization of the particularities of that particular society. By a combination of sheer literary skill and a seemingly endless inventiveness, Sōseki contrived to maintain the vitality of his book throughout eleven chapters and some quarter million words: but one understands why, eventually, he had no choice but to drown his hero. It would, however, be unreasonable to denigrate the first-rate satire of the later parts of *I Am a Cat* simply because they lack the full felinity, the quite exceptional beguilement, of the earlier parts of the book. Moreover, one has only to read Sōseki's other comic novel *Botchan (The Young Master),* of 1906, with its entirely human style of human satire, to realize that, however much humanity seeps in to soften the later portions of *I Am a Cat,* even their most un-catlike passages contain that glint, that claw-flash under velvet, which stamp them ultimately aluroid.

In the Introduction to *Ten Nights of Dream* we mentioned the difficulties that face any translator of Sōseki's work by reason of his individual literary style: its reflection of his deep scholarship in Chinese, Japanese and English literature, its consequent exploitation of a singularly wide range of reference and its unique combination of classical and colloquial language. We accordingly thought it reasonable to give a brief explanation of our approach to the problems of translating Sōseki's prose and, in particular, we referred to John Wyclif's comments on "defaute in untrewe translatynge." Further experience of Sōseki's idiosyncratic brilliance has only confirmed our belief in the wisdom of Wyclif's advice to translators that "whann chaungyng of wit is foundun, amende they it as resoun wole." For the characteristics of Sōseki's literary style (and the translating difficulties that derive therefrom) naturally become more marked as he increasingly drew upon his wide and sophisticated resources in order to maintain the impetus of his original inspiration. Indeed, in making the present translation of four further chapters of *I Am a Cat,* we found it increasingly necessary to fill in for Western readers that background of Oriental reference and culture which, in the original, naturally did not need to be explained to a Japanese audience. Many translators supply such background information in the form of notes but, in the conviction that an annotated novel is only a little less nauseating than an annotated poem, we have so constructed our version that, while it departs along Wyclifian lines from strict literal accuracy, it does, we trust, both flow acceptably in English (an English trans-

lation, as Jowett once implacably remarked, must be in English) and at the
same time properly convey the literary
substance of its Japanese original.

There are, world-wide, impressive pre-
cedents for this approach. That most
familiar in the English-speaking world is
the King James version of the Holy Bible.
Those most pertinent in the Oriental
context are the translations into Chinese
made by Kumarajiva (343–413) of the
Sanskrit originals of the basic texts of
Buddhism. Kumarajiva's translations were
attacked by contemporary and subsequent
critics on the grounds that, unlike the
slightly earlier literal versions of the same
material by Tao An (312–385) and the
considerably later versions by Yen Tsung
(557–610), Kumarajiva's texts were demonstrably inaccurate in that, if put back
into Sanskrit, the consequent retro-trans-
lations would differ markedly from the
Sanskrit originals. We would rest our
defense of our own use of Kumarajiva's
style of translation both on fact (which
should appeal to literalists) and on legend
(which usually reflects a deeper truth than
literalists are willing to acknowledge). The
fact is that Kumarajiva's versions of the
Buddhist texts became the versions which
underlie all subsequent development of
Buddhist thought and practice in the Far
East, while the griping voices that spoke

in support of Tao An and Yen Tsung are now no more than faint dust-whispers in the drier gulches of Academe. The legend is, to us, even more persuasive. "If," wrote Kumarajiva, "these words of the Buddha have been by me correctly rendered into the Chinese language, then let not my tongue be burnt at the time of my cremation." It was, they say, found unconsumed among his ashes.

—THE TRANSLATORS

Note: Japanese names throughout this book, except on the cover and title page, are given family name first in the Japanese style.

I T HAS become my usual practice to sneak into the Goldfields' mansion.

I won't expand upon the meaning of my use of "usual," which is merely a word expressing the square of "often." What one does once, one wants to do again, and things tried twice invite a third experience. This sense of enquiry is not confined to humanity, and I must ask you to accept that every cat born into this world is endowed with this psychological peculiarity. Just as in the human case, so with cats: once we've done a thing more than three times over, the act becomes a habit and its performance a necessity of our daily life. If you should happen to wonder why I so often visit the Goldfield place, let me first address a modest enquiry to mankind. Why do human beings breathe smoke in through the mouth and then expel it through the nose? Since such shameless inhalation and exhalation can do little to ease the belly's hunger and less to cure giddiness, I do not see why a race of habitual smokers should dare to offer criticism of my calls on the Goldfields. That house is my tobacco.

To say that I "sneak in" gives a misleading 13

impression: it sounds vaguely reprehensible, a term to be used for the self-insinuations of thieves and clandestine lovers. Though it is true that I am not an invited guest, I do not go to the Goldfields' in order to snitch a slice of bonito or for a cozy chat with that disgusting lapdog whose eyes and nose are convulsively agglomerated in the center of its face. Hardly! Or are you suggesting that I visit there for the sheer love of snooping? Me, a detective? You must be out of your mind! Among the several most degrading occupations in this world, there are, in my opinion, none more grubby than those of the detective and the money-lender. It is true that once, for Coldmoon's sake, I displayed a chivalrous spirit unbecoming in a cat and kept an indirectly watchful eye on the Goldfields' goings-on. It was but once that I acted with such ill-placed kind-heartedness, and since that isolated occasion I have done nothing whatever that could bring a twinge to the conscience of the most pernickety cat. In which case, you may ask, why did I describe my own actions with such an unpleasantly suggestive phrase as "to sneak in"? I have my own good reasons, but their explanation involves analysis in depth.

In the first place it is my opinion that the sky was made to shelter all creation, and that the earth was made so that all things created able to stand might have something to stand on. Even those human beings who love argument for the arguing's sake could surely not

deny this fact. Next we may ask to what extent
did human effort contribute to the creation
of heaven and earth; and the answer is that
it contributed nothing. What right, then,
do human beings hold to decide that things
not of their own creation nevertheless belong
to them? Of course the absence of right need
not prevent such creatures from making that
decision, but surely there can be no possible
justification for them prohibiting others from
innocent passage in and out of so-called
human property. If it be accepted that Mr.
So-and-so may set up stakes, fence off sections
of this boundless earth and register that area
as his own, what is to prevent such persons
from roping off blue sky, from staking claims
on heaven, an enclosure of the air? If natural
law permitted proprietorial parceling-out of
the land and its sale and purchase at so much
the square foot, then it would also permit
partition of the air we breathe at so much the
cubic unit and its three-dimensional sale. If,
however, it is not proper to trade in sky, if
enclosure of the empyrean is not regarded as
just in natural law, then surely it must follow
that all land-ownership is unnatural and irrational. That, in fact, is my conviction:
therefore I enter wherever I like. Naturally
I do not go anywhere where I do not want to
go: but, provided they are in the direction I
fancy, all places are alike to me. I slope
along as it suits me, and feel no inhibition
about entering the properties of people like
the Goldfields if I happen to want to. How-

ever, the sad fact is that, being no more than a cat, I cannot match mankind in the crude matter of simple physical strength. In this real world the saying that "Might is right" has very real force; so much so that no matter how sound my arguments may be, the logic of cats will not command respect. Were I to press the argument too far, I should be answered, like Rickshaw Blacky, with a swipe from a fishmonger's pole. In situations where reason and brute force are opposed and one may choose either to submit by a perversion of reason or to achieve one's reasonable ends by outwitting the opposition, I would, of course, adopt the latter course. If one is not to be maimed with bamboo poles, one must put up with things: one must press on. Thus, since the concept of trespass is irrational, and since "sneaking in" is only a form of "pressing on," I am prepared to describe my visits as sneaking in.

Though I have no wish whatever to spy upon the Goldfields, inevitably, as the number of my visits mounts, I get to know things about that family which I'd rather not have known and I see happenings which, willy-nilly, I cannot purge from my memory. I am, for instance, regretfully aware that when Madam Conk dabs water on her face she wipes her nose with inordinate care; that Miss Opula persistently gluts herself on rice-cakes dusted with bean-flour; and that old man Goldfield, in striking contrast with his wife, has a nose as flat as a pancake. Indeed, not just his nose, but his whole face is flat.

It is a face so leveled one suspects that when
he was a lad he must have got into a fight
with the strong-boy of some children's gang
who, grabbing him by the scruff of the neck,
rammed his face so hard against a plaster-wall
that even now, forty years on, his squashed
and crumpled features are a living memento
of that unlucky day. Though it is certainly
an extremely peaceful, even a harmless, face,
it is somewhat lacking in variety. However
much that face becomes infuriated, still it
stays flat. I came to learn, moreover, that
old man Goldfield likes tuna-fish, sliced and
raw; and that whenever he eats that delicacy,
he pats himself on his own bald pate with a
plashy, pattering sound. Further, because his
body is as squat as his face is flat, he affects
tall hats and high-stepped wooden clogs;
facts which his personal rickshawman finds
so vastly entertaining that he's always yatter-
ing on about them to the houseboy who, for
his part, finds such sharp accuracy of observation impressively remarkable. I could go on
forever with such details of the Goldfields'
goings-on.

It has become my practice to enter the
garden by the back-gate and to survey the lie
of the land from the cover of a small artificial
mound helpfully constructed there for dec-
orative purposes. Having made sure that
everything is quiet and that all the paper-
windows are slid shut, I gingerly creep forward and hop up onto the veranda. But if

I hear lively voices or consider there's a risk that I might be seen from within, I mosey off eastward round the pond, nip past the lavatory and finish up, safe and unobserved, under the veranda. My conscience is in no way troubled, I've nothing to hide and no reason to be scared of anything whatever; but I've learnt what to expect if one should have the vile ill-luck to run up against one of those lawless and disorderly bipeds. Were the human world cram-jammed with robbertoughs as violent as that long-departed villain, Kumasaka Chōhan, then even the most illustrious and virtuous of men would act as cautiously as I do. Inasmuch as old man Goldfield is a dignified sort of businessman, I wouldn't expect him to come after me with any such dirty great sword, five feet three of it they tell me, as Kumasaka was wont to brandish. However, from what I've seen and heard, Goldfield has his own unpleasant quirks and is certainly not disposed to accept that a man's a man for a' that. If Goldfield's overbearing with his fellowmen, how would he treat a cat? A cat, as I keep on saying, is also a cat for a' that; but given Goldfield's nature, even a feline of the most upright virtues would be wise to adopt a low posture and a very cautious attitude once inside the Goldfield premises. This very need to be constantly on the *qui vive* is, I find, delightful; and my taste for danger explains why I make these frequent risky visits. I will give further and careful thought to this fascinating point; and, when I have completed my analysis of cat-mentality, I will publish the results.

What's up today, I wonder, as I settle my chin against the grass on top of the garden-hillock and survey the prospect spread below me. The doors of their ample drawing-room are open wide to the full spring day and I can see, inside, the Goldfields busily engaged in conversation with a guest. I am somewhat daunted by the fact that Madam Conk's pro-boscis is pointed directly in my direction: it glares across the pond straight at my unpro-tected forehead. This is my first experience of being glared at by a nose. Facing his guest, old man Goldfield presents himself to my gaze in full profile. My eyes are spared one half of his flattened features but, for the same profilic reason, the location of his nose is indeterminable; and it is only because one can see where his grayish-white moustache sprouts raggedly from the flesh that one can deduce that the vent-holes of his nostrils must be gaping closely thereabove. I amuse myself with the reflection that the light spring breeze might well blow on forever if it encountered no more formidable obstruction than that jutless physiognomy. Of the three, the Goldfields' guest has the most normal fea-tures but, precisely because of their regularity, there's no facial peculiarity I see reason to point out. For anything to be regular sug-gests that the thing's all right; but regularity can be so utterly regular as to become, by its very ulteriority, mediocre and of no account. Which is extremely pitiable.

I wonder who he is, this unfortunate fellow fated to be born in this glorious reign behind so meaningless a phiz. My curiosity can't be satisfied unless I crawl more close and, in my accustomed manner, establish myself underneath the veranda and listen to what is said. So under it I go.

". . . and my wife actually took the trouble to call on the man to ask for information." As usual, old man Goldfield speaks in an arrogant manner. The manner is certainly prideful, but his voice contains no hint of sharpness. It gives, like his face, an impression of massive flatness.

"I see. So he's the fellow who used to teach your Mr. Avalon Coldmoon. I see, I see. Yes, yours is a good idea. . . . Indeed, I see." This guest is positively overflowing with "I see's."

"But somehow my wife's approaches all proved pretty pointless."

"No wonder. Sneaze is not strong on point. Even in the days when he and I shared digs and looked after ourselves, his lack of point, his lack of resolution, were painfully extreme. You must," he said, turning to Madam Conk, "have had a difficult time."

"Difficult! That's hardly the word. Never in my life have I made a visit and been so badly treated." As is her ugly custom,

Madam Conk snorts storm-winds down her
snout.

"Did he say anything rude to you? He's
always been obstinate, a real old stick-in-the-
mud. He's been teaching that English Reader
for years without a break, so you can imagine . . ." With what charm and tact this
guest is making himself agreeable.

"He is beyond help. I understand that
every time my wife asked a question, she
received a blunt rebuff."

"What impudence! As I see it, persons of
some small education tend to grow conceited
and, if they happen also to be poor, their
characters become as bitter as sour grapes.
Indeed some people in that condition turn
truly quite absurd. For no reason at all,
they flare up at persons of wealth as if unconscious of their own total ineffectiveness.
It's quite astonishing how they behave; as if
the rich had robbed them personally of things
they never owned." The guest's laughter
rang out affectedly, but he certainly seems
delighted with himself.

"Scandalous behavior! It's because they
know nothing of the world that they carry on
so outrageously. So I thought I'd have him
taken down a peg or two. It's time he learned
how many beans make six."

"I see. Splendid. That should have shaken
him up a bit. Done him no end of good."
Goldfield is smothered in his guest's con-
gratulations, even though that sycophant

still lacks the least idea of the kind of rod which Goldfield's put in pickle for poor Sneaze.

"But really, Mr. Suzuki, Sneaze is impossible. D'you know," said Madam Conk, "down at his school he won't exchange two words with our friend, Mr. Fukuchi. Nor, come to think of it, with Mr. Tsuki either. We'd thought he'd learnt his lesson and was keeping quiet because he knew he's been sat on; but, would you believe it, only the other day we heard he'd been chasing after our harmless houseboy with a walking-stick! Just imagine that. He's a man of thirty. No sane grown-up could act in such a way. Perhaps," she ended hopefully, "despair has driven him dotty."

"But what can have driven him to such an act of violence?" Their guest seems mystified that Sneaze could act so firmly.

"Nothing much really. It seems that our houseboy happened to be passing Sneaze's place, made some innocent remark and, before you could say Jack Robinson, Sneaze came rushing out in his bare feet and began lashing around with his stick. Whatever the houseboy may have said, he is, after all, no more than a boy. But Sneaze is a bearded man and, what's more, supposed to be a teacher."

"Some teacher," says the guest.

"Some teacher," echoed Goldfield.

It would seem that this precious trio has reached complete agreement that, if one hap-

pens to be a teacher, one should, like some
wooden statue, grin and bear whatever insults
anyone cares to offer.

"And then," said Madam Conk, "there's
that fibbing crank called Waverhouse. I've
never heard a man tell such a stream of whop-
pers. All quite pointless, but all flat lies.
Really, I've never clapped eyes on such a
loony in my life."

"Waverhouse? Yes, he seems to be brag-
ging on as usual. Was he also there when you
called on Sneaze? He, too, can be a tricky
customer. He was another of our group in
digs. I remember I was always having rows
with him on account of his incessant ill-
judged mockery and his warped sense of
humor."

"A man like that would rile a saint. We
all, of course, tell lies, sometimes out of
loyalty, sometimes by demand of the occasion; and in such circumstances anyone may
fairly bend the truth. But that man Waverhouse tells his lies for no good reason at all.
What can one do with a man like that? I just
can't see how he brings himself to rattle off
such reams of barefaced balderdash. What
does he expect to gain by it?"

"You've hit the nail on the head. There's
nothing one can do when a man tells lies for
a hobby."

"I made a special visit to that miserable
house to ask no more than the normal questions about Avalon that any mother would,
but all my efforts came to nothing; they

vexed me and they put me down. But all the same, I felt obliged to do the decent thing; so afterward I sent our rickshawman around with a dozen bottles of beer. Can you imagine what happened? That saucy usher Sneaze had the cheek to order our man to take the bottles away because, so he said, he saw no reason why he should accept them. Our fellow pressed him to take the bottles as a token of our appreciation. So then Sneaze said that he liked jam but reckoned beer too bitter. Then he just shut the door and went off back to his room. Now can you beat that? How damned rude can one get?"

"That's terrible." The guest seems, this time genuinely, to think it's really terrible.

After a brief pause I hear the voice of old man Goldfield. "And that's, in fact, precisely why we've asked you here today. It's something, of course, to make fun of that fool Sneaze behind his back, but that sort of thing doesn't entirely suit our present purpose. . . ." Splash, spatter; spatter, spatter, splash. He's patting his pate as though he's just been eating sliced, raw tuna-fish. Of course, being tucked away underneath the veranda, I cannot actually see him beating that wet tattoo on the skin of his hairless head but I've seen so much of him lately that, just as a priestess in a temple gets to recognize the sound of each particular wooden gong, so I can tell, from the quality of the sound, even though I'm under the floor, when old man Goldfield takes to drumming on his skull.

assistance in this matter. . . ."

"If I can be of any service, please don't
hesitate to ask me. After all, it's entirely due
to your kind influence that I have had the
great good fortune to be transferred to the
Tokyo office." Their guest is so obviously
anxious to oblige that he must be another of
those many persons under obligation to
return some form of Goldfield help. Well,
well, so the plot thickens. I wandered out
today simply because the weather was so
wonderful, and I certainly had not expected to
stumble upon such exciting news of planned
skulduggery. It is as though one had gone
to the family temple dutifully intending to
feed the Hungry Dead, only to find oneself
invited to a right old lash-up of rice-cake
dumplings and bean-paste jam in the private
room of a priest. Wondering what kind of
assistance will be sought from this client-
guest, I prick my ears to listen.

"Don't ask me to explain it, but that nit-
witted teacher keeps planting crazy notions
in the noddle of young Coldmoon: like, for
instance, hinting that he shouldn't marry any
daughter of mine." He turned to his wife.
"That's what he hinted, didn't he?"

"Hinting's not the word. He said flat out
'No one in his senses would ever marry a
daughter of that creature. Coldmoon,' he
said, 'you simply mustn't marry her.'"

"Well, blow me down. Did he really have
the brazen cheek to speak of me as a crea-

ture? Did he really pitch it strong as that?"

"Not half he didn't. The wife of the rickshawman came round double-quick just to be sure I knew."

"Well, there you are, Suzuki. That man Sneaze is getting to be a nuisance, wouldn't you agree?"

"How extremely irritating. Marriage negotiations are not matters in which to meddle lightly. Surely even a dunderhead like Sneaze ought to have the common sense to know that. Really, the whole thing's beyond my comprehension."

"In your undergraduate-days you lived in the same boarding-house as Sneaze; and, though things may have changed by now, I understand that you two then used to be pretty pally. Now, what I want you to do is to go and see Sneaze and try to talk some reason into him. He may be feeling offended: but if he is, it's really all his own fool fault. If he plays ball, I'd be willing to give him generous help with his personal affairs; and we would, of course, lay off annoying him. But if he keeps on gumming things up the way he's so far done, it will only be natural if I find ways of my own to settle his meddlesome hash. In short, it just won't pay him to go on acting obstinate."

"How very right you are. Continued resistance on his part would be idiotic. It could bring him no possible profit and could well cause him loss. I'll do my best to make him understand."

"One more thing. Since there are many other suitors for our daughter, I can't make any firm promise of giving her to Coldmoon; but you could usefully go so far as to hint that, if he studies hard and gets his degree in the near future, he stands a chance of winning her."

"That should encourage him to buckle down to study. All right, I'll do as you wish."

"One last thing. It may sound odd, but what especially sticks in my gullet is the way that Coldmoon, who's supposed to be so smart, laps up everything that Sneaze lets drop; and even goes round addressing that crack-brained ninny as though he were some kind of sage professor. Of course, since Coldmoon's not the only man we are considering for Opula, such unbecoming conduct is not of vast importance. Nevertheless . . ."

"You see," squawked Madam Conk, butting in on her husband's careful sentence, "it's just that we're sorry for Coldmoon."

"I've never had the pleasure of meeting the gentleman but, since to marry into your distinguished family would be to ensure a lifetime's happiness, I'm quite convinced that he himself could not possibly wish other than the marriage."

"You're absolutely right," said Madam Conk. "Coldmoon's keen to marry her. It's only that numbskull Sneaze and his crackpot crony Waverhouse who keep throwing spanners in the works."

"Most reprehensible. Not the style of

behavior one expects from any reasonable, well-educated person. I'll go and talk with Sneaze."

"Please do: we'd be most grateful. Remember, too, that Sneaze knows better than anyone else what Coldmoon's really like. As you know, during her recent call my wife failed to dig out anything much worth knowing. If, in addition to ascertaining details of his scholastic talent and all that stuff, you could also find out more about Coldmoon's character and conduct, I'd be particularly obliged."

"Certainly. Since it's Saturday today, Sneaze must be home by now. Where does he live, I wonder," says Suzuki.

"You turn straight right from our place, then turn left at the end of the road. About one block along, you'll see a house with a tumble-down black fence. That," said Madam Conk, "is it."

"So it's right here in this neighborhood! Then it should be easy. I'll go and see him on my way home. It will be simple to identify the house by the name-plate."

"You may, or you may not, find his name-plate on display. I understand he uses one or two grains of cooked rice to stick his visiting-card on his wooden gate. When it rains, of course, the cardboard comes unstuck. Then on some convenient sunny day he'll paste another card in place. So you can't be sure that his name-plate will be up. It's hard to see why he keeps to such a troublesome routine when the obvious thing to do is to hang up a wooden name-board. But that," sighed Madam Conk, "is just another example of his general cussedness."

"Astonishing," remarked Suzuki, "but I'll find the place in any case by asking for the house with the black fence in a state of disrepair."

"Oh yes, you'll find it easily enough. There's not another house in the whole neighborhood quite so filthy-looking. Wait a minute! I've just remembered something else. Look for a house with weeds growing out of the roof. It's impossible to miss."

"In fact, a quite distinguished residence," said Suzuki and, laughing, took his leave.

It would not suit my book to have Suzuki beat me home. I've already overheard as much as I need to know; so, still concealed beneath the veranda, I retrace my steps to the lavatory where, turning west, I briefly break cover to get back behind the hillock and, under its concealment, regain the safety of the street. A brisk cat-trot soon brings me to the house with the weed-grown roof where, with the utmost nonchalance, I hopped up onto our own veranda.

My master had spread a white woolen blanket on the wooden boards and was lying there, face-down, with the sunshine of this warm spring day soaking into his back. Sunshine, unlike other things, is distributed fairly. It falls impartially upon the rich and the poor. It makes a squalid hut, whose only distinctions are the tufts of shepherd's purse sprouting from its roof, no less gaily warm than, for all its solid comfort, the Goldfields' mansion. I am, however, obliged to confess that that blanket jars with the day's spring feeling. No doubt its manufacturer meant that it should be white. No doubt, too, it was sold as white by some haberdasher specializing in goods imported from abroad. No less certainly my master must have asked for a white blanket at the time he bought it. But all that happened twelve or thirteen years ago, and since that far-off Age of White the blanket has declined into a Dark Age where its present color is a somber gray. No doubt the passage of time will eventually turn it black, but I'd be surprised if the thing survived that long. It is already so badly worn that one can easily count the individual threads of its warp and woof. Its wooliness is gone and it would be an exaggeration, even a presumption, to describe this scrawny half-eroded object as a blanket. A "blan," possibly; even a "ket"; but a full-blown "blanket," no. However, my master holds, or at least appears to hold, that anything which one has kept for a year, two years, five years, and eventually for a decade, must then be kept for the rest of one's natural life. One would think he were a gypsy. Anyway, what's he doing, sprawled belly-down on that remnant of the past? He lies with his chin stuck out, its jut supported on a crotch of hands, with a lighted cigarette projecting from

doing. Of course inside his skull, deep below
the dandruff, universal truths may be spin-
ning around in a shower of fiery sparks like
so many Catherine Wheels. It's possible but,
judging from his external appearance, not
likely even in one's wildest imaginings.

The cigarette's lit tip is steadily burning
down and an inch of ash, like some gray
caddis-case, plopped down onto the blanket.
My master, ignoring that declension, stares
intently at the rising smoke. Stirred by the
light spring breeze, the smoke floats up in
loops and vortices, finally to gather in a kind
of clinging haze around the ends of his wife's
just-washed black hair. Gentle reader, please
accept my apologies. I had completely forgotten to mention that lady's presence.

Mrs. Sneaze is sitting so that her bottom
presents itself before her husband's face. You
think that impolite? Speaking for myself, I
would not call it so. Both courtesy and
discourtesy depend on one's point of view.
My master is lying perfectly at ease with his
cupped face in close proximity to his wife's
bottom: he is neither disturbed by its proximity nor concerned at his own conduct. His
wife is equally composed to position her
majestic bum bang in her husband's face.
There is neither the slightest hint nor intention of discourtesy. They are simply a much-
married couple who, in less than a year of
wedlock, sensibly disengaged themselves from
the cramps of etiquette. Mrs. Sneaze seems

to have taken advantage of the exceptionally fine weather to give her pitch-black hair a really thorough wash with a concoction made from raw eggs and some special kind of seaweed. Somewhat ostentatiously, she has let her long straight hair hang loose around her shoulders and all the way down her back; and sits, busy and silent, sewing a child's sleeveless jacket. In point of fact, I believe it is purely because she wants to dry her hair that she's brought out here both her sewing-box and a flattish cushion made from some all-woolen muslin; and it is similarly to present her hair at the best angle to the sun that, deferentially, she presents her bottom to her spouse. That's my belief, but it may of course be that my master moved to intrude his face where her bum already was.

Now, to return to that business of the cigarette smoke, my master lay watching with fascinated absorption the way in which the smoke, floating upward through his wife's abundant and now loosened hair, was itself combed into an appearance of filaments of blue-gray air. However, it is in the nature of smoke to go on rising, so that my master's fascination with this singular spectacle of hair-entangled smoke compels him, lest he miss any phase of its development, steadily to lift his gaze. His eyes, first leveled on her hips, move up her back, over her shoulders and along her neck. And it was after his concentrated stare had completed the ascent of her neck and was focused on the very crown of her head that he suddenly let out an involuntary gasp of surprise.

For there, on the very summit of the lady whom he had promised to love and cherish till death did them part, was a large round patch of baldness. That unexpected nakedness, catching the clear spring sunshine, threw back the light and shone with an almost braggart self-confidence. My master's eyes remain fixed open in surprise at this dazzling discovery and, disregarding the danger of such brightness to his own uncovered retinal tissue, he continues to goggle at her skin's bright mirror. The image that then immediately shot into my master's mind was of that dish on which stood the taper set before the altar in the household shrine handed down in his family for untold generations. My master's family belongs to the Shin sect of Buddhism, a sect in which it is the established custom to lay out substantial sums, more indeed than most of its adherents can afford, on household shrines. My master suddenly remembers how, when he was a very small boy, he first saw the shrine in the family safe-room. It was a miniature shrine, somber though thickly gilded, in which a brass taper-dish was hanging. From the burning taper a faint light shone, even in the day-time, on the rounded dish. Bright against the shrine's general darkness, that image of the shining dish, seen in his childhood time and time again, leapt back into his mind as he gaped at his wife's bald patch. But that first remembrance quickly vanished; to be replaced by memories of the pigeons at the Kannon Temple in Asakusa. There seems no obvious connection between temple doves and Mrs. Sneaze's gleaming scalp, but in my master's mind the association of images is clear and very close. It, again, is an association deriving from his early childhood. Whenever then he was taken to that temple, he would buy peas for the pigeons. The peas cost less than a farthing a saucer. The saucers, made of an unglazed reddish clay, were remarkably similar, both in size and color, to his wife's bare patch.

"Astonishingly similar." The words escape from his lips in tones of an awed wonder.

"What is?" says his wife without even turning toward him.

"What is? There's a big bald patch on the crown of your head. Did you know?"

"Yes," she answers, still not interrupting her sewing. She seems not the least embarrassed by his discovery. A model wife, at least in point of imperturbability.

"Was it there before we married or did it crop up later?" Though my master does not come out with an open accusation, he clearly sounds as if he would regard himself as having been tricked into marriage if the bald patch was, in fact, present in her maidenhood.

"I don't remember when I got it. Not that it matters. Whatever difference could a bald patch make?" Quite the philosopher, isn't she just.

"Not that it matters! But it's your own hair that we're talking about." My master speaks with a certain sharpness.

"It's just because it is my own hair that it doesn't matter." An effective answer, but she may have been feeling slightly self-conscious for she lifted her right hand gently to stroke the spot. "Oh dear," she said, "it's got much bigger. I hadn't realized that." Her tone conceded that the patch was larger than would be normal at her age and, now driven onto the defensive, she added "Once one starts doing one's hair in the married style, the strands at the crown come under a very real strain. All married women lose hair from the top of the head."

"If all married women lost hair at your rate, by the time they were forty they'd be bald as kettles. You must have caught some kind of disease. Maybe it's contagious. You'd better go round and have it looked at by Dr. Amaki before things go too far," says my master, carefully stroking his own head.

"That's all very well, but what about you? White hairs in your nostrils! If baldness is contagious, white hairs will be catching." Mrs. Sneaze begins to go over to the attack.

"A single white hair in the nostrils is obviously harmless, and it doesn't even show. But fox-mange on the crown of the head cannot be ignored. It is, especially in the case of a young woman, positively unsightly. It's a deformity."

"If you think I'm deformed, why did you marry me? It was you who wanted the marriage, yet now you call me deformed. . . ."

"For the simple reason that I didn't know. Indeed I was unaware of your condition until this very day. If you want to make an issue of it, why didn't you reveal your naked scalp to me before we got married?"

"What a silly thing to say! Where in the world would you find a place where girls had to have their scalps examined before they could get married?"

"Well, the baldness might be tolerable but you're also uncommonly dumpy; and that is certainly unsightly."

"There's never been anything hidden about my height. You knew perfectly well when you married me that I'm slightly on the short side."

"Of course I knew, but I'd thought you might extend a bit; and that's why I married you."

"How could anyone grow taller after the age of twenty? Are you trying to make a fool of me? Eh?" She drops the sleeveless jacket and, twisting around to face her husband, gives him a threatening look as if to say "Now watch your step: you go too far, and you'll be sorry."

"There is surely no law forbidding people from growing taller after the age of twenty. I cherished a faint hope that, if I fed you up on decent food, you might prolong yourself."

With every appearance of meaning what he said, my master was about to develop his curious reasoning, when he was cut off by a sharp ringing of the door-bell followed by a loud shout of "Hello." Snuffling after the scent of that shepherd's purse on the roof, the dogged Suzuki seems at last to have tracked down Sneaze's den.

My master's wife, temporarily postponing their domestic row, snatches up the jacket and her sewing-box and vanishes into an inner room. My master scrabbles his gray blanket up into a ball and slings it into the study. The maid brings in the visitor's card and gives it to my master; who, having read it, looks a little surprised. Then, having told the maid to show the visitor in, he goes off into the lavatory with the card still clasped in his hand. If it is beyond one's comprehension that he should thus suddenly take to the loo, it is even more difficult to explain why he should have taken with him the visiting-card of Suzuki Tōjūrō. It is, in any case, very hard luck on the soul of that visiting-card that it should have to accompany him to that noisome place.

The maid deposits a printed-cotton cushion on the floor in front of the alcove-recess, invites the guest to be seated in that place of honor and then removes herself. Suzuki first inspects the room. He begins by examining the scroll displayed in the alcove: its Chinese characters, allegedly written by

Mokuan, that master calligrapher of the Zen sect, are, of course, faked, but they state that flowers are in bloom and that spring is come to all the world. He next turns his attention to some early-flowering cherry-blossoms arranged in one of those celadon vases which they turn out cheap in Kyoto. Then, when his roving glance chances to fall upon the cushion provided for his particular convenience, what should he find but, planted serenely smack in its center, a squatting cat. I need hardly add that the cat in question is my lordly self.

It was at this point that the first quick tremor of tension, a ripple so small it did not show on his face, quaked in Suzuki's mind. That cushion had undoubtedly been provided for himself but before he could sit down on it, some strange animal, without so much as a by-your-leave, had dispossessed him of the seat of honor and now lay crouched upon it with an air of firm self-confidence. This was the first consideration to disturb the composure of his mind. In point of fact, had the cushion remained unoccupied, Suzuki would probably have sought to demonstrate his modesty by resting his rump on the hard mat-floor until such time as my master himself invited its transfer to the comfort of the cushion. So who the hell is this that has so blithely appropriated the cushion which was destined, sooner or later, to have eased Suzuki buttocks? Had the interloper been a human being, he might well have given way. But to

be pre-empted by a mere cat, that is intolerable. It is also a little unpleasant. This minor
animality of his dis-sedation was the second
consideration to disturb the composure of
Suzuki's mind. There was, moreover, something singularly irritating about the very
attitude of the cat. Without the least small
twitch-sign of apology, the cat sits arrogantly
on the cushion it has filched and, with a cold
glitter in its unamiable eyes, stares up into
Suzuki's face as if to say "And who the hell
are you?" This is the third consideration to
ruffle Suzuki's composure. Of course if he's
really irked, he ought to jerk me off the
cushion by the scruff of my neck. But he
doesn't. He just watches me in silence. It is
inconceivable that any creature as massive
and muscular as man could be so afraid of
a cat as not to dare to bring crude force to
bear in any clash of wills. So why doesn't
Suzuki express his dislike by turfing me off
the cushion with summary dispatch? The
reason is, I think, that Suzuki is inhibited by
his own conception of the conduct proper
to a man. When it comes to the use of force
any child three feet tall can, and will, fling
me about quite easily: but a full-grown man,
even Suzuki Tōjūrō, Goldfield's right-hand
man, cannot bring himself to raise a finger
against this Supreme Cat Deity ensconced
upon the holy ground of a cotton cushion
two feet square. Even though there were no
witnesses, a man would regard it as beneath
his dignity to scuffle with a cat for possession

of a cushion. One would make oneself ridiculous, even a figure of farce, if one degraded oneself to the level of arguing with a cat. For Suzuki, the price of this human estimate of human dignity is to endure a certain amount of discomfort in the nates: but, precisely because he feels he must endure it, his hatred of the cat is proportionately increased. When, every now and again he looks at me, his face exudes distaste. Since I find it amusing to see such wry distortion of his features, I do my best myself to maintain an air of innocence and resist the temptation to laugh.

While this pantomime was still going on, my master left the lavatory and, having tidied himself up, came in and sat down. "Hello," he said. Since the visiting card is no longer in his hand, the name of Suzuki Tōjūrō must have been condemned to penal servitude for life in that evil-smelling place. Almost before I could feel sorry for the visiting card's ill-luck, my master, saying "Oh, you!" grabs me by the scruff of my neck and hurls me out to land with a bang on the veranda.

"Do take this cushion. You're quite a stranger. When did you come up to Tokyo?" My master offers the cushion to his old friend and Suzuki, having turned it catside-down, dumps himself upon it.

"As I've been so busy I haven't let you know, but I was recently transferred back to our main office in Tokyo."

"That's splendid. We haven't seen each

other for quite a long while. This must be the
first time since you went off to the provinces?"

"Yes, nearly ten years ago. Actually I did
sometimes come up to Tokyo, but as I was
always flooded with business commitments, I
simply couldn't manage to get round to see
you. I do hope you won't think too badly of
me. But, unlike your own profession, a business firm is honestly very busy."

"Ten years make big changes," observes
my master, looking Suzuki up and down.
His hair is neatly parted. He wears an En-
glish-made tweed suit enlivened by a gaudy
tie. A bright gold watch-chain glitters from
his waistcoat. All these sartorial touches
make it hard to credit that this can really be
one of Sneaze's friends.

"Well, one gets on. Indeed I'm now virtually obliged to sport such things as this. . . ."
Suzuki seems a little self-conscious about the
vulgarly fashionable display of his watch-
chain.

"Is that thing real?" My master poses his
question with the minimum of tact.

"Solid gold. Eighteen carat," Suzuki answers, smilingly smug. "You, too," he continued, "seem to have aged. Am I right in
thinking you've children now? One? Am I
right?"

"No."

"Two?"

"No."

"What, more? Three, then, is it?"

"Yes, I have three children now, and I don't know how many more to come in the future."

"Still as whimsical as ever. How old is your eldest? Quite big, I suppose."

"Yes, I'm not quite sure how old, but probably six or seven."

Suzuki laughed. "It must be pleasant to be a teacher, everything so free and easy. I wish I too had taken up teaching."

"Just you try. You'd be sorry in three days."

"I don't know. It seems a good kind of life: refined and not too stressful, plenty of spare time and the opportunity really to study one's own special interest. Being a business-man is not bad, either, though at my present level things aren't particularly satisfactory. If one becomes a businessman, one has to get to the top. Anywhere lower on the ladder, you have to go around spouting idiotic flat-teries and drinking *saké* with the boss when there's nothing you want less. Altogether, it's a stupid way of life."

"Ever since my school-days I've always taken a scunner to businessmen. They'll do anything for money. They are, after all, what they used to be called in the good old days: the very dregs of society." My master, with a businessman right there in front of him, indulges in tactlessness.

"Oh, have a heart. They aren't always like that. Admittedly, there's a certain coarseness about them; for there's no point in even trying to be a businessman unless your love for money is so absolute that you're ready to accompany it on the walk to a double suicide. For money, believe you me, is a hard mistress and none of her lovers are let off lightly. As a matter of fact, I've just been visiting a businessman and, according to him, the only way to succeed is to practice the 'triangled technique': try to escape your obligations, annihilate your kindly feelings, and geld your-self of the sense of shame. Try-an-geld. You get it? Jolly clever, don't you think?"

"What awful fathead told you that?"

"He's no fathead. Smart as a whip, in fact. And increasingly respected in business circles. I rather fancy you know him. He lives up a side-street just around the corner."

"You mean that frightful Goldfield?"

"Goodness me, but you're really getting worked up. He only meant it, you know, as a kind of joke. It's simply a way of summariz-ing the fact that to make money one must go through hell. So please don't take a joke too seriously."

"His 'triangled technique' may, I grant, be a joke: let's say it's screamingly funny. But what about his wife and her nauseating nose? If you've been to their house you could hardly have avoided colliding with that beak."

"Ah, Mrs. Goldfield. She seems a sensible woman of broad understanding."

"Damn her understanding. I'm talking

about her nose. Her nose, Suzuki; it's a positive monstrosity. Only the other day I composed a *haitai* poem about it."

"What the dickens is a *haitai* poem?"

"Do you mean to say you've never heard of the current experiments in the composition of extended *haiku?* You do seem cut off from what's going on in the world."

"True. When one is as busy as I am, it's absolutely impossible to keep up with things like literature. Anyway, even when a lad, I never liked it much."

"Are you aware of the shape of Charlemagne's nose?"

"You are indeed in a whimsical mood." Suzuki laughed quite naturally. "Of course I haven't the faintest idea of the shape of Charlemagne's nose."

"Well, what about Wellington then? His troops used to call him Nosey. Did you know that?"

"Why on earth are you so batty about noses? Surely it doesn't matter if a nose happens to be round or pointed."

"On the contrary, it matters very much. D'you know about Pascal?"

"Questions, questions! Am I supposed to be taking an exam or something? No, I don't know about Pascal. What did he do?"

"He had this to say."

"What to say?"

" 'Had Cleopatra's nose been a little bit shorter, the history of the world would have been changed.' "

"Did he now!"

"Perhaps now you see why one can't afford to underestimate the importance of noses."

"All right, I'll be more careful in future. By the way, I dropped in today because there's something I'd like to ask you. It's about a chap you used to teach. Avalon something or other. I can't remember his other name, but I understand that you and he see a lot of each other."

"You mean Coldmoon?"

"That's it, Coldmoon. Well, I've really come to make enquiries about him."

"About a matrimonial matter?"

"One might say that. You see, I called in earlier on the Goldfields. . . ."

"The Nose herself came sniffing round here only the other day."

"Did she? Well, as a matter of fact she mentioned that she'd called. She said she'd paid a visit in order to present her respects to Mr. Sneaze and to entreat his assistance in a matter of information, but that Waverhouse was present and made so many and such frivolous interruptions that she just got muddled."

"It was all her own fault. Coming round here with a nose like that."

"She spoke of you with the deepest respect. She's just regretful that the performance put on by Waverhouse made it impossible to ask you certain personal questions about Coldmoon, and she has therefore asked me to speak on her behalf. For what it's worth, I've never before played the part of an honest broker in matters of this sort: but if the two parties most directly concerned are not against the idea, it's not a bad thing to serve as a go-between and so bring about a marriage. Indeed, that's the reason for my present visit."

"How kind of you to call," commented my master somewhat acidly. But, though he could not explain his feeling, he was inwardly a little moved by that phrase about "the two parties most directly concerned." Its slightly sentimental appeal made him feel as though a wraith of cool air had drifted through his sleeves on a hot and humid summer's night. It is true that my master's character is based on so firm an inborn bedrock of cold reserve and obstinacy that he is, by nature, one of this world's wet blankets. Nevertheless his nature is of a completely different type from that of the vicious, heartless products of modern civilization. The antique mold of his nature is clearly evidenced in the way in which he flares up at the slightest provocation. The sole reason for his barney with Madam Conk was that he could not stand her modern-day approach. But his flat dislike of the mother was no fault of her daughter. Similarly, because he abominates all businessmen, he finds Goldfield acutely distasteful: yet here again, no blame can be laid on the daughter. Sneaze bears no real ill-will toward her, and Coldmoon is his favorite pupil and

he loves that lad more deeply than he would
a brother. If Suzuki is correct in his statement
that the two parties most directly concerned
do, in fact, love each other, then it would be
an act unworthy of a gentleman even indirectly to hinder true love's course. Sneaze
is quite convinced that he himself is a gentleman, so his only remaining question is whether Coldmoon and Miss Goldfield are in
love. He must, if he is to amend his attitude,
first be sure of the facts.

"Tell me, does that girl really want to
marry Coldmoon? I don't care what Goldfield or the Nose feel about the matter, but
what are the girl's own feelings?"

"Well, you see . . . that is, I understand . . .
well, yes, I suppose she does." Suzuki's
answer is not exactly clear-cut. Thinking that
all he had to do was to find out more about
Coldmoon, he came unbriefed on Opula's
view of the match; so even this slippery lad
now finds himself in a bit of a jam.

"The word 'suppose' implies some measure
of uncertainty." My master, tactless as ever
and not a man to be put off, goes in again like
a bull at a gate.

"True enough. Perhaps I should have
expressed myself more clearly. Now, the
daughter certainly has a certain inclination.
Indeed, that's true. What? Oh yes, Mrs.
Goldfield told me so herself, though I gather
she sometimes says some awful things about
Coldmoon."

"Who does? D'you mean the daughter?"

"Yes."

"What impudence! That snip of a girl disparaging Coldmoon! Well, it can hardly mean that she cares for him."

"But that's just it. Odd you may think it, but sometimes people do run down precisely those they love."

"I can't conceive that anyone could be so deranged as to behave like that." Such intricate convolutions of human nature are quite beyond my master's blunt and simple mind.

"In fact the world is full of such people. Certainly that's how Mrs. Goldfield interprets her daughter's comments. She said to me 'My daughter must be quite taken with that young Coldmoon, for I've even heard her say he looks like a bewildered gourd.' "

These revelations of the strangeness of the human heart leave my master dumbstruck. Wide-eyed and wordless, he stares in astonishment at Suzuki as though he were some soothsayer wandered in from the street. Suzuki seems to have the nous to sense the danger implicit in my master's unbelief and, fearful lest further discussion should wreck his whole approach, quickly changes the subject to aspects of the matter which even my master cannot fail to understand.

"Consider these facts," he said. "With her good looks and money that girl can marry almost where she chooses. Now Coldmoon may be a splendid fellow but, comparing their relative social positions . . . No, such

comparisons are always odious and could be
taken as offensive. So let me put it this way:
that, in terms of personal means, the couple
are obviously ill-matched. Surely then, you
can see that if the Goldfields are so worried
that they ask me to come round here and
talk to you, that very fact indicates the
strength and nature of their daughter's yearnings?" One can't deny Suzuki's clever. He is
relieved to notice that my master seems impressed by his latest line of argument but,
realizing that the question of the degree of
bleeding in Miss Goldfield's heart is likely to
be re-opened if he allows the conversation to
loiter on her feelings about Coldmoon, he
concludes that the best way to complete his
mission is to drive the discussion forward as
quickly as possible.

"So, you see, as I've just explained, the
Goldfields aren't expecting money or property: what they'd like instead is that Coldmoon should have some status of his own,
and by status they mean the public recognition of qualification that is symbolized in a
senior degree. It's not that they're so stuck-up
as to say that they'll only consider giving him
their daughter if he holds a doctorate. You
mustn't misunderstand them. Things got
jumbled up the other day when Mrs. Goldfield called on you purely because Waverhouse chose to amuse himself with his usual
display of verbal fireworks and distorting
mirrors. No, no, please don't protest. I know
it was none of your fault. Mrs. Goldfield

49

吾輩は猫である

spoke in admiration of you as a frank and honest man. I'm certain that the blame and any awkwardness that may have arisen must be laid at Waverhouse's door. Anyway, you see, the nub of the matter is this: if Coldmoon can get a doctorate, he would have independent status. People would naturally look up to Dr. Coldmoon, and the Goldfields would be proud of such a son-in-law. So what are the chances of Coldmoon's making an early submission of his thesis and receiving his doctorate? You see, so far as the Goldfields themselves are concerned, they'd be the last to demand a doctor's degree: they wouldn't even ask for a bachelor's. But they have to consider what the world and his wife will say, and when dealing with the world one simply cannot be too careful."

So presented, the Goldfields' request for a doctorate seems not altogether unreasonable; and anything he deems not altogether unreasonable qualifies for my master's support. He feels inclined to act as Suzuki suggests. Suzuki, it is clear, can twiddle my master around his artful little finger. I recognize my master as indeed a simple honest man.

"Well, in that case, next time Coldmoon drops around, I'll urge him to get on with his thesis. However, I feel that I must first question him closely to ascertain whether or not he really wants to marry that Goldfield girl."

"Question him closely! If you act with such meticulous formality, the business will

never get settled. The quickest way to a happy
ending is to sound his mind, casually, in the
course of an ordinary conversation."

"To sound his mind?"

"Yes, but perhaps the word 'sound' is not
quite right since it can be thought to smack of
indirection. Of course I'm not suggesting
deception of any kind. What I mean is that
you would understand the drift of his mind
in this matter from simply talking with him
about generalities."

"You might understand, but I wouldn't
unless I ask him point-blank."

"Ah well, I suppose that's up to you. But
I don't think it would be reasonable to ruin a
romance by slinging cold water on it, quite
unnecessarily and even for fun, like Waverhouse. Perhaps one doesn't need actually to
jostle them into marriage, but surely in matters of this sort, the two parties most directly
concerned should be left undistracted by ir-
relevant outside influences to settle their
future for themselves. So next time Coldmoon calls, try, please, not to interfere. Of
course I don't mean you yourself. I'm referring to Waverhouse: nobody emerges scathe-
less whom Waverhouse discusses." Since
Suzuki could not very well speak ill of my
master, he spoke thus bitterly against Waverhouse, when, talk of the devil, who should
come floating unexpectedly in on a spring
breeze through the kitchen but Waverhouse
himself.

"Hello," he said, throwing the accent onto

the second syllable, "a visitor from the past! I haven't seen you in years. You know," he rattled on, "Sneaze treats intimate friends like me with scant ceremony. Shocking behavior! One ought to visit him roughly once a decade. Those sweets, for instance; you wouldn't get those if you called here often." Scanting all ceremony, Waverhouse reaches over and crams his mouth with a large piece of red-bean sugar-paste confection from the well-known Fujimura shop. Suzuki fidgets. My master grins. Waverhouse munches. As from the veranda I watched this interlude, I realized that good theater need not depend upon speech, that high dramatic effect can be achieved with mime. The Zen sect practices instantaneous mental communication of truth from mind to mind in dialogues of silence. The dumb show going on within the room is, no doubt, a version of that practice; and the dialogue, though brief, is pretty sharply worded. It was, of course, Waverhouse who broke the silence.

"I'd thought, Suzuki, that you'd become a bird of permanent passage, always coming or going somewhere, but I see you've landed back. The longer one lives, the greater the chance that something odd will turn up." Waverhouse babbles away to Suzuki with that same complete absence of reserve which characterizes his conversations with my master. Though they lodged together in their student days, still it would be normal for a man to address someone whom he hasn't seen for at least ten years with a little more formality. Except when that man is Waverhouse. That he pays not the least regard to the requirements of convention marks him out as either a superior soul or a rightdown jobbernowl. But which one cannot say.

"That's a little hard. Aren't you being a trifle pessimistic," commented Suzuki noncommittally: but his way of fingering his watch-chain betrayed a continuing unease.

"Tell me, have you ever ridden on a tram?" My master shot this sudden and peculiar enquiry at Suzuki.

"It seems that I've come here today simply to provide you two city-wits with a laughing-stock on which to hone your singular sense of humor. Though it's true that I'm very much up from the provinces, I actually happen to own some sixty shares in the Tram Company of your precious city."

"Well, that's not to be sneezed at! I myself once used to own eight hundred and eighty-eight and a half of them. But I'm sorry to say that the vast majority have now been eaten by insects, so that I've nothing but one single half-share left. If you'd come up to Tokyo a little bit earlier, I would gladly have given you some ten shares that, till very recently, the moths had not yet got at. What a sad misfortune."

"I see you haven't changed your personal style of ridicule. But joking apart, you're bound to do well if you just hang on to stocks of that quality. They cannot fail, year after year, to climb in value."

"Quite right: even half a share, provided one holds it for roughly a thousand years, will end up making you so rich you'll need three strongrooms. You and I, razor-minded fellows with our senses keyed to the economic inwardness of these stirring times, are, of course, keenly conscious of the significance of stocks. But what about poor Sneaze? Just look at him. To him," said Waverhouse, conferring on my master a look of withering pity, "stocks are no more than some vague kind of gillyflower." He helped himself to another piece of confectionery. His appetite is contagious, for my master, too, stretches out his arm toward the sweet-dish. It is in the immutable nature of the human world that positivity should triumph, that initiative be aped.

"I do not care two hoots about stocks or shares, but I do wish poor old Sorosaki had lived to ride, if only once, on a tram." With morose concentration my master studies the pattern cut by his teeth in his half-eaten sweet.

"Had Sorosaki ever got into a tram, sure as eggs is eggs, he'd have finished up at the end of the line in Shinagawa. He was an absent-minded man. He's better off where he is now, engraved upon a weight-stone as Mr. the-late-and-sainted Natural Man. At least he knows where he is."

"I'd heard that Sorosaki had died. I'm sorry. He was a brainy chap," says Suzuki.

"Brainy, all right," Waverhouse chipped in, "but when it came to cooking rice he was a positive imbecile. Every time it came round to Sorosaki's turn to do the cooking, I contrived to keep body and soul together by eating out on noodles."

"True, Sorosaki's rice had the peculiar characteristics of smelling burnt yet being undercooked. I, too, used to suffer. What's more, he had an odd way with the accompanying bean-curds. Uncooked and so cold that one could not eat them." Suzuki dredges up a grievance ten years old.

"Even in those days Sneaze was Sorosaki's closest friend. They used to trot off together every evening to gulp down rice-cakes swamped in red-bean soup; and, as a proper and inevitable result, Sneaze is now a martyr to dyspepsia. As a matter of fact, since it was Sneaze who always guzzled most, he should by rights have predeceased his crony."

"What extraordinary chains of logic do run round in your contraption of a mind. Anyway," remarked my master, "there was nothing particularly reprehensible about my going out for sweet-bean soup. As I remember it, your own evening expeditions took the form of haunting a graveyard in order to beat up tombstones with a bamboo stick. You called it physical exercise, but that didn't save you from a right old rap on the knuckles

when the priest came out and caught you."
In this exchange of student reminiscence I
thought my master's counter-swipe with the
tombstones far more telling than that dribble
of soup from Waverhouse. Indeed, by his
laughter, Waverhouse himself acknowledged
the defeat.

"Indeed," he said, "I well remember that
priest. He told me I was thumping on the
noddles of the dear departed, which would
disturb their sleep. So would I please desist.
All I did was to make some practice passes
with a bamboo wand; but General Suzuki
here, training his body with wrestlers' drills,
engaged those stones in violent personal
combat. I recall that on one occasion he
wrestled loose and overthrew three monu-
ments of assorted sizes."

"That did annoy the priest. He got quite
fierce about it, insisting I restore my victims
to their original positions. I asked him to
hold his horses for a moment while I went
and hired some navvies for the job; but he
wouldn't hear of it. 'Navvies,' he said, 'won't
do. Only your own hands can purge the evil
they have done. The dead will accept no
penitence but yours.' "

"And what a sight you were! Moaning and
groaning through those muddy puddles in a
calico shirt and a loincloth tied with string
. . ."

"And I remember you, with what a coldly
serious face you stood and sketched me as I
struggled with those goddam stones. Such

utter heartlessness. I'm very slow to anger, but at that time, from the bottom of my heart, I ached to kill you for your insultingly dispassionate detachment. I can still remember what you said that day. Can you, I wonder?"

"How could anyone remember what was said ten years ago. I do, however, recall the words engraved on one of the stones: Returning Fountain Hall, Lord Yellow Crane the Great Deceased, January 1776. The stone, moreover, was antique and elegant. I was tempted to make off with it. Its general style was Gothic and chimed entrancingly with those aesthetic principles I cherish." Waverhouse is off again, flaunting his gimcrack knowledge of aesthetics. Whoever heard of Japanese Gothic from 1776. . . .

"That's as may be; but listen to what you said. These are your very words. 'Since I propose to devote my days to the study of aesthetics, I must, for future reference, grasp each and every opportunity to set down upon paper any event of interest in this universe which comes before my eyes.' What's more, you were kind enough dispassionately to add 'A man such as I, one totally and exclusively committed to the pursuit of learning, cannot permit himself the luxury of such personal feelings as those of pity or compassion.' I could have done you in for such nonchalance. But all I did in fact was to grab your sketch-book with my muddied hands and rip the thing to ribbons."

"And it was from precisely that moment

that my talent as a creative artist, up till then widely accepted as remarkably promising, was nipped in the bud, never to bloom again. I have my own whole skeleton of bones still to pick with you."

"Don't be so daft. If anyone's entitled to a grudge, it's me."

"Waverhouse, from as far back as my mind can reach, has always been a windbag." My master, having munched his sweet to extinction, rejoins the conversation. "He never means what he says and has never been known to keep a promise. Pressed hard for an explanation, he never apologizes but trots out endless pretexts and prevarications. Once when the myrtles were in bloom in the temple yard, he told me that he would complete a treatise he was writing, on those same old cherished principles of aesthetics, before the flowers fell. 'Impossible,' I said. Can you guess his answer? He claimed, despite appearances, to be of iron will. 'If you doubt my word,' he said, 'just name your bet.' I took him up on it and we agreed that the loser should stand a dinner at a Western restaurant over in Kanda. I took the bet because I was certain that he'd never get his writing done in time; but I confess that, not in fact having the cash to pay for the dinner if I lost, I remained a little nervous that he still might work a miracle. Anyway, he showed no signs of getting down to work. A week went by, three weeks went by and still he hadn't written a single page. At last the flowers of the myrtle fell and, though the tree stood empty, Waver-house stood calm. Looking forward to my Western meal, I pressed our friend to meet his obligation. Not to put too fine a point upon his answer, he told me to get lost."

"No doubt," chimed in Suzuki, "he offered this, that and the other reason?"

"Indeed he did, the barefaced rogue. You can't imagine how obstinate he was. 'Say what you will,' he said, 'about my other flaws and faults. I admit them all, and readily. But the fact remains that in strength of will I'm stronger than the pack of you.'"

"Do you mean," asked Waverhouse himself, "that, having written nothing, I still claimed not to have lost the bet?"

"Of course you did. You said the bet was not about finishing the treatise but about your iron will. And in respect of that iron quality, so you most willfully informed me, you would yield to none. You conceded that your memory might be poor; so poor indeed that you had next day forgotten that you intended to write a paper on the principles of aesthetics; but you maintained that your will to write it remained ferric to the core. The fault lay in your memory, not in your will. So, though the myrtle-flowers were fallen and the treatise still unwritten, you made it pain-fully clear that you saw no reason why you should come across with my dinner."

"Now that's very interesting. And so very typical of Waverhouse." I can't see what in that rather tedious story should so particularly interest Suzuki, but the tone of his comments is markedly different from that which he used before Waverhouse came in. Perhaps such variousness is a sign of a clever man.

"Not in the least interesting." My master interjects a sharpish contradiction.

"It distresses me that you should still be feeling so put out about it; but is it not for that very reason that I've had men out with lanterns searching high and low for those peacocks' tongues I promised you? Don't be so huffy, Sneaze. Just wait a while and all shall be made up. Incidentally, this talk about writing a treatise reminds me that I've called today with some especially odd news."

"Since you bring round odd news every time you visit, I'll take that statement with a pinch of salt."

"But today's odd news truly is sensational. Cross my heart and hope to die, it's stunning. Coldmoon's started writing his thesis. What about that? Since in his own quaint way Coldmoon has a fairly elevated opinion of himself, I wouldn't have expected him to engage in such a mundane, tasteless chore as getting a thesis actually written: but it appears that he, too, is tainted with wordly ambition. Now don't you think that odd? You'd better let that Goldfield woman know that she may now start dreaming of decking her family-tree with a full-blown doctor of acorns."

At the first mention of Coldmoon's name, Suzuki begins jerking his chin and twitching his eyes at my master in silent pleas that nothing should be said of their recent conversation. My master fails to notice these entreating galvanisms. A short while back, under the suasion of Suzuki's moral lecture, he had felt sufficiently sorry for the love-lorn daughter not to indulge his unabated antipathy toward her mother. But as soon as Waverhouse referred to Madam Conk, his recollection of his recent row with that virago came flooding back in full spate. That the row had had its comic aspects did not make it any the less provoking. But the news that Coldmoon had started to write his thesis, that was really marvelous. He was grateful to Waverhouse, who had more than fulfilled his boast of having something startling to say, for bringing such a welcome present. It was, indeed, a stunning piece of news; stunning but singularly pleasant. It doesn't greatly matter, one way or the other, whether Coldmoon marries the girl: but it is certainly an excellent thing for the lad to get his doctorate. In surprising ways my master knows himself, and would with absolute humility accept that not a tear need fall if a botched wooden statue is left undecorated to rot away in some dark back-corner of a sculptor's shop. But when a statue is superbly carved, when its basic quality is noble, then no effort should be spared and no time wasted in ensuring that it be given gilding of appropriate splendor.

"Are you really telling me that Coldmoon's

started writing?" my master enquires eagerly and paying no attention at all to the jittering Suzuki.

"What a suspicious mind you've got! Don't you ever believe what I tell you? Yes, he's started; but I regret I cannot tell you whether his thesis will be concerned with the Stability of Acorns or with the Mechanics of Hanging. Whatever the subject, a Coldmoon thesis must be a glorious snub for the Nose."

Suzuki has been getting more and more restive as Waverhouse repeats and develops his discourteous references to Madam Conk; but Waverhouse, not noticing, sails unconcernedly on.

"I have," he said, "carried out some further research into noses and am happy to advise you of an interesting treatment of the subject in the *Life and Opinions of Tristram Shandy, Gentleman*. Had Sterne but known of that mountain of relevant material, how greatly it would have helped him. The sadness of chronology! To think that that staggering organ, eminently qualified as it is to gain immortal nose-fame, should be born, like many another nosegay, to blush unseen! One's heart is filled with an immense compassion. When next it thrusts itself upon us, I shall sketch that vast promontory of flesh for my future reference in the study of aesthetics." There's no restraining Waverhouse.

"But I hear that the Goldfield girl is yearning to be Coldmoon's bride." My master makes a fair summary of Suzuki's representa-

tions, while the latter, annoyance twitching
from every feature on his face and electric
messages flashing from his eyes, signals
desperately for disengagement. My master,
like some nonconducting substance, remains
immune to these distraught discharges.

"How bizarre. It strains the mind to think
that the daughter of such a man might fall
in love. . . . Not, I would imagine, that it
could be love of any quality: just rubbing
noses."

"Whatever its nature," my master commented, "let's hope that Coldmoon marries
her."

"What's that?" said Waverhouse. "Who's
now hoping Coldmoon marries her? Only
the other day you were dead against such a
disastrous match. Have you gone soft or
something?"

"It's not a matter of going soft. I never go
soft, but . . ."

"But something's happened? That's it,
isn't it? Now look here, Suzuki, since you're
some kind of lower life-form in the business
jungle, let me give a piece of advice to guide
your future slitherings. It's with reference to
that grunting Goldfield and his piglet daughter. The idea that reasonable persons might
be called upon to treat that creature with the
respect due to the wife of Mr. Avalon Coldmoon, that talented national figure; why,
man, the thing's impossible. They'd no more
balance each other than would a paper-
lantern and a big bronze bell. No one who

calls himself a friend to Coldmoon could stand by and not speak against the folly of such a misalliance. Surely, Suzuki, even you, looking at it as a businessman, can see the sense in what I'm saying."

"What a kerfuffle you do still manage to kick up! Always something stirring, eh? You haven't changed one little bit in all of these ten years. Really, it's remarkable." Suzuki tries to slither round the question.

"Since you compliment me as being re-remarkable, let me display some more remarkable dollops of learning appropriate to this case. The ancient Greeks set very high store by physical prowess and encouraged its pursuit by awarding valuable prizes to the winners of all sorts of athletic contests. But, strangely enough, there is no record that they ever offered prizes for intellectual prowess. Until recently this curious circumstance incessantly puzzled me."

"I see," says Suzuki still trying to make himself agreeable. "That does seem odd."

"However, just the other day, I chanced, in the course of my researches into aesthetics, to light upon the explanation. Years of accumulated worrying fell instantly away from me and, in that blessed trice, as though disburdened of all errors and earthly delusions, I found myself transported to that pure realm of infinite enlightenment where my soul rejoiced in its transcendence of the world and its attainment of pansophic self-awareness." Waverhouse departs on such a

flight of gongoristic drivel that even the
toadying Suzuki allows his face to slip into
the lineaments of having had enough. "He's
at it again" may be read in my master's resigned expression as, with eyes cast down, he
sits there tapping, *kan-kan-kan,* on the rim
of the cake-dish with his ivory chopsticks.
Nowise disconcerted, Waverhouse blathers
on.

"And to whom do you think we are indebted for that brilliant logical analysis
which, by its simple explanation of this
seeming anomaly, has rescued us forever
from the dark abyss of doubt? It was that
famous Greek philosopher, the greatest of
all scholars since scholarship began, the
renowned founder of the Peripatetic School,
Aristotle himself. His explanation—I say,
Sneaze, please stop flogging that cake-dish
and pay a little more attention—may be
summarized thus. The prizes awarded at
Greek contests were worth more than the
performances that earned them, for the prizes
were intended not only to stimulate effort but
to reward achievement. Consequently if one
were to give a prize for intellectual prowess,
for knowledge itself, one would have to find
something to award which was more valuable
than knowledge. But knowledge already is
the rarest gem in the world. The Greeks,
unwilling to debase the value of knowledge,
piled up chests all crammed with gold to the
height of Mount Olympus. They gathered in
the wealth of Croesus, and wealth beyond

that wealth; but in the end they recognized that the value of knowledge cannot be matched, let alone exceeded. So, masters of reason that they were, they decided that the prize should be nothing at all. From this, Suzuki, I trust you will have learnt that, whatever the color of your money, it is worthless stuff compared with learning. Let us accordingly apply this revealed truth, this fundamental principle, to the particular problem that has arisen today. Surely you're bound to see that Goldfield's merely a paper man, a bill of exchange with eyes and a nose scrawled onto it. If I may put it epigrammatically, the man's no more than an animated banknote. And if he's money in motion, currency one might say, his daughter's nothing but a circulating promissory note. In contrast, now, let us consider Coldmoon. With consummate ease he graduated with the best degree of his year from the highest seat of learning in our land. On leaving the Imperial University, he showed no sign of slackening of effort: on the contrary, fiddling with the antique fastening-strings of his short surcoat, he devotes himself, both day and night, to intensive study of the thorny problem of the stability of acorns. And in addition to all that, this indefatigable servant of learning is just about to publish a thesis which, unquestionably, will embody intellectual concepts beside whose depth, originality and scope those adumbrated by the great Lord Kelvin must pale into insignificance. It is true he was concerned in an abortive attempt at suicide, but that was no more than a passing fancy of a kind common among lads of spirit. Certainly the incident can cast no serious doubt upon his reputation as a vast repository of learning and intelligence. If I may adapt to Coldmoon's case one of my own earlier turns of phrase, I should describe him as a circulating library. He is a high-explosive shell, perhaps only a twenty-eight centimeter, but compactly charged with knowledge. And when at the properly chosen time this projectile makes its impact upon the world of learning, then, if it detonates, detonate it will."

Waverhouse, unbelievably, seems to have run out of steam. Confused by his own jumble of metaphors, he almost flinches and his flow of language peters pointlessly out. As the saying goes, the dragon's head of his opening remarks has dwindled down to a snake's tail of an ending. However, though Waverhouse may falter, he's unlikely to shut up. In a matter of seconds he's off again.

"In that inevitable explosion things like promissory notes, though there be thousands of them, will all be blasted into dust. It follows that, for Coldmoon, such a female simply will not do. I cannot consent to so ill-suited an alliance. It would be as though an elephant, that wisest and most noble of all animals, were to marry the greediest piglet of a greedy farrow." With a final burst of speed Waverhouse breasts the tape. "That's-so-isn't-it-Sneaze?" My master, silent, resumed his melancholy tapping on the cake-dish.

Looking a bit depressed and obviously at his wit's end for a suitable answer, Suzuki mumbles something about not being able entirely to agree. His position is, indeed, delicate. His hands, as it were, are still wet with blood from his verbal assassination, barely a half-hour back, of Waverhouse's character; and a man as outrageously tactless as my master might, at any moment, come straight out with anything. Suzuki's soundest tactic is to receive, and if possible smother, the Waverhouse attack; and then, in the general confusion, to wriggle away to safety as quickly as he can. Suzuki's clever. Very much a man cast in the modern mold, he seeks to avoid head-on collisions and considers it positively medieval to enter into arguments that, of their nature, can have no practical result. In his opinion the purpose of life is not to talk, but to act. If events develop as one wishes, then life, its purpose thus fulfilled, is good: but if events not only develop as one wishes but do so without difficulties, fret or altercation, then life, its purpose slitheringly fulfilled, is paradisal. Suzuki's unwavering devotion to this Elysian principle of slithering had brought him great success in the business world he'd entered after graduating from the university. It had brought him a watch of eighteen-carat gold. It had brought him a request from the Goldfields that he should do them a small favor.

It had even enabled him to maneuver Sneaze nine-tenths of the way toward doing what the Goldfields wished. Then Waverhouse descends upon the scene. Out of the ordinary, careless of all conventions, totally eccentric, he manifests himself as an incarnation of capriciousness operating in accordance with a psychological pattern never previously observed in the human creature. No wonder that Suzuki feels a bit bewildered. Though Suzuki's principle was invented by a variety of clever gentlemen seeking success in Meiji circumstances, its prime practitioner is Suzuki Tōjūrō himself, and it is consequently he who is most signally stumped when the principle proves inapplicable.

"It's only because you're out of your depth," Waverhouse pressed on, "that you sit there looking supercilious and offer no more useful contribution than the cool comment that you can't entirely agree. But if you'd been here the other day when that Nose came throwing her weight around, even you, businessman to the backbone though you are, even you would have felt like throwing up. It's true, Sneaze, isn't it? Go on, tell him. I thought you handled the situation magnificently."

"But I'm told," my master almost smirked, "that my conduct on that occasion created a more favorable impression than did yours."

The answering laugh was a mixture of pity and scorn. "What incredible self-confidence! I begin to understand how you manage to sail along at school unperturbed by the mockery of your colleagues and your pupils' shouts of Savage Tea. In matters of will-power I'm a match for anyone: but when it comes to sheer nerve, I'm just not even in your class. I humble myself in the presence of such staggering self-confidence."

"Why on earth should I be moved by such puerile carryings-on? Their grumbles don't scare me. Though Sainte-Beuve was perhaps the greatest of all critics, his lectures at the Sorbonne proved so unpopular that, whenever he walked in the streets, he was obliged to carry a dagger up his sleeve to defend himself against attacks from students. Similarly, when Brunetière's lectures attacked the novels of Zola . . ."

"Come off it, Sneaze. You're not a professor or a university lecturer. For a mere teacher of the English Reader to start comparing himself with world-famous professors is like a minnow demanding to be treated as a whale. If you keep on saying things like that, you're bound to be laughed at."

"That's just your opinion. As I see it, Sainte-Beuve and I, considered as scholars, are of roughly the same standard."

"What fantastic self-esteem! But if I were you, I'd give up any idea of going around with a dagger. You might cut yourself. Of course, if university professors do go armed with dirks, it might be reasonable for a teacher of the English Reader to carry a folding penknife. But even so, any edged tool is dangerous. What you ought to do is to toddle along to the Nakamise arcade down in Asakusa and get yourself a toy pop-gun. You could carry it slung from your shoulder. You'd make a charming picture. What d'you think, Suzuki?"

Suzuki's feeling better. Relieved that the conversation has at long last veered away from the subject of the Goldfields, he feels it safe to venture a few, and preferably flattering, sentences.

"As it always was, it's been great fun to take part again in such a lively but good-natured discussion. Not having seen you two for a full ten years, I feel as though I had just walked back into a spacious sunny landscape out of some dark and narrow alley. As you'll understand, conversations among business associates tend to be pretty tricky. One has to watch one's step, constantly minding one's p's and q's, and ever alert for a stab in the back. The never-ending worry and strain is genuinely painful. But I myself enjoy frank and open conversation, and it's marvelous to be talking again with one's student-chums in the same old style of uninhibited honesty. I'm delighted that my visit brought me the added and unexpected pleasure of running into Waverhouse. Well," he concluded, "I must leave you now. I've got a man to meet."

Having delivered himself of these slithery sentences, Suzuki was beginning to lever himself loose from my cushion, when Waverhouse remarked "I'll come along too. They're waiting for me at the Entertainment Temperance Union over in Nihombashi. Let's run along together."

"Fine," said Suzuki. "Part of the way we'll be going in the same direction." So, arm in arm, they left.

TO WRITE down every event that takes place during a period of twenty-four hours and then to read that record would, I think, occupy at least another twenty-four hours. Though I am all in favor of realistically descriptive literature, I must confess that to make a literal record of all that happened in a day and a night would be a *tour de force* quite beyond the capacities of a cat. Therefore, however much my master's paradoxical words and eccentric acts may merit being sketched from life at length and in exhaustive detail, I regret that I have neither the talent nor the energy to set them all down for my readers. Regrettable as it is, it simply can't be helped. Even a cat needs rest.

After Suzuki and Waverhouse had taken their departure, it became as quiet as a night when winter's icy wind suddenly drops and the snow falls soundlessly. My master, as usual, shuts himself up in his study. In their six-mat sleeping-room, side by side in a bumpy row, the children lie asleep. Mrs. Sneaze in the adjoining room, a room that faces south, lies in bed giving suck to Menko, her year-old baby daughter. It has been a hazy day of the type we often get in springtime, and dusk has fallen early. The sound of wooden clogs passing in front of the house can be heard quite distinctly in the living-room and the sound of a Chinese flute, played in random snatches by someone in the boarding-house on the next street, falls lullingly in broken drifts upon my sleepy ears. Outside it must still be hazy. Having filled my stomach with that dinner of rice with fish gravy which O-san had provided in my abalone-shell, I feel that a little shut-eye is precisely what I need.

It has come to my ears that *haiku*-poets have taken to using the phrase "cat's love" as a means of indicating that a poem is concerned with the season of spring. Indeed, I have myself observed that there are nights in early spring when my fellow-cats in this neighborhood set up such a caterwauling that sleep is well-nigh impossible. As it happens, I personally have not yet experienced such a derangement of my senses. Nevertheless, love is a universal stimulant. It is the way of all things, from Olympian Zeus right down to the very humblest of the earthworms and mole-crickets that chirrup on this earth, to wear themselves out in this exhausting field of endeavor. It is, therefore, only natural that cats too, dreamily joyful, should indulge themselves in the risk-fraught search for love. Indeed, on looking back, I remember that I myself once pined away for love of Tortoise-shell. I hear that even Opula, that gorman-

dizer of rice-cakes dusted with bean-flour, that
daughterly extension of the very base-line of
the triangled technique, old man Goldfield, I
hear that even she is smitten with love for the
unlikely person of Coldmoon. I consequently
would not dream of sneering at those tom
cats and their lady-consorts who, throughout
the whole wide world, are so inspired by the
ineffable magic of these evenings of the
spring that they run amuck under the ex-
cruciations of their lusts and loneliness. However, and to my infinite regret, even when
invited to participate, I just don't have the
urge. In my present condition all that I need
is rest. I am so utterly sleepy that I simply
couldn't perform. Accordingly I sidle slug-
gishly around the children's bedding, set paw
on that forbidden territory at the end where
their own feet lie and, finding a suitable
space, curl up comfortably and drop off into
slumber.

I happen to open my eyes and, looking
round, find that my master is lying asleep
inside the bedding spread beside his wife's.
When he goes to bed, it is his invariable
habit to bring along some small Western
book from his collection; but I've never seen
him actually read so much as two consecutive
pages. Sometimes he just brings the book,
places it beside his pillow and makes no
faintest attempt to read it. Though it seems
peculiarly unnecessary to bring a book of
which not one line will be read, such actions
are quite typical of my master. However

much his wife laughs at him, however sua-
sively she begs him to give up this stupid
habit, still he persists. Every evening he
makes a point of going to bed with a book
which he does not read. Sometimes he makes
a positive beast of himself and shuffles in
with three or four books tucked under his
arms. For several days until a little while ago
it was his nightly practice to tote in Webster's
whacking great dictionary. I suppose this
behavior reflects some kind of psychological
ailment. Just as some men of peculiarly
extravagant taste can only get to sleep to the
gentle simmering singing of one of Ryūbun-
dō's special iron kettles, so too, perhaps, my
master cannot sleep without a book beside
his pillow. It would seem that for my master
a book is not a thing to be read but a device
to bring on slumber: a typographical sleep-
ing-pill, a paginated security-blanket.

I take a peep to see what he's brought
tonight and find that he's fallen asleep with
a slim red volume lying half-open on his chin
with its top edge almost brushing his moustache. Judging by the fact that his left-hand
thumb is sandwiched between the pages, he
must tonight have made a praiseworthy improvement on his usual performance to the
extent of reading at least a line or two. Beside
the bed, in its accustomed place, its cold gray
surface a dull reflection of this warm spring
night, his nickel watch lies gleaming.

My master's wife, the nursling baby
tumbled about a foot away from her, lies

open-mouthed and snoring. Her head
has slipped down from the pillow. In my
opinion, there is nothing more unbecoming
in the human type than its indecent habit of
sleeping with the mouth left open. Never in
a lifetime would a cat be caught in such
degenerate conduct. The mouth and the nose
have their separate functions: the former is
provided for the making of sounds and the
latter for respiratory purposes. However, in
northern lands the human creature has
grown slothful and opens its mouth as seldom
and as little as possible: one obvious result of
this muscular parsimony is that northern
style of tight-lipped speech in which the
words would seem to be enunciated through
the nostrils. That is bad; but it's even worse
when the nose is kept closed and the mouth
assumes the respiratory function. The result
is not only unsightly but could indeed, when
rat-shit drops from the rafters, involve real
risk to health.

As for the children, they too, small-scale
reproductions of the indignities of their
parents, lie sprawled about on their bedding.
Tonko, the elder daughter, as if to demonstrate the monstrous regiment of elder
sisters, lies with her right arm stretched out
full so that her fist is firmly planted against
her sister's ear. In a kind of sleeping counter-
attack, Sunko lies flat on her back with one
leg flung across her elder's stomach. Both
have managed to revolve through ninety
degrees since, properly positioned, they

drifted off to sleep; but, perfectly at ease in their unnatural dispositions, they slumber deeply on.

There is something peculiarly moving about the faint illumination of a night-lamp in the dark hours of the spring. Over the unpretentious but sadly inelegant interior-scene of our dwelling it casts a flickering radiance so sweet and gentle that it seems to be inviting our gladdest marvelment at the beauty of this night. Wondering what the time is, I look around the room. Dead silence reigns, broken only by the ticking of the wall-clock, the snores of Mrs. Sneaze and, despite the distance, the relentless grinding of the servant's teeth. Whenever they tell that O-san woman of her grinding ways, she swears it isn't true. Obstinately, flatly, she takes her oath that, never from the day since she was born, not that many babies turn up tusked, has she ever ground a tooth. She neither apologizes nor attempts to break the habit; just stubbornly insists that she doesn't remember ever having done such a thing. Since she does it in her sleep, it's probably true that she doesn't remember doing it. But facts, remembered or not, are all, alas, still facts. There are persons in this world who, having perpetrated villainies, remain assured of their own absolute saintliness. They really do convince themselves that they're pure of any guilt. Such utter self-deception is, I dare say, a form of simple-mindedness: but however genuine the self-deception, if the actuality is objectionable

to other people it should be put down. As I
lay there thinking that there's no real difference between our grinding skivvy and those
evil-doing gentlefolk who think themselves
so righteous, the night wore peacefully on.

Suddenly I hear a light double-tapping on
the wooden shutters of the kitchen entrance.
Odd. People would hardly come visiting at
this time of the night. It must be one of those
damnable rats. So let it bump. As I mentioned earlier, I long ago decided never to
catch rats. Then, once again, I heard a
double-tapping. Somehow it doesn't sound
like a rat. If it is a rat, it must be an extremely
cautious one. For the rats in my master's
house, like the students at his school, devote
their entire energies, both day and night, to
the practice of riotous behavior and seem to
believe that they were only brought into this
world to disrupt as violently as possible the
dopey dreamings of that pitiable man. No rat
of ours would make such modest noises. No,
it is not a rat. Far too timid. The other night
we had a rat come boldly into my master's
bedroom, nip off a snippet from the tip of
his already stunted nose and then depart in
squeaking triumph. It just can't be a rat. As
if to confirm my suspicions, the next sound
that I hear is the scraping creak of the
wooden shutter being lifted from its groove;
and then I hear the sliding screen being eased
sideways as quietly as possible. Beyond all
doubt, it's not a rat. It can then but be human.
Even Waverhouse or Suzuki would hesitate

at this late hour to lift the latch and walk in unannounced; and neither, I think would go so far as to dismantle a wooden shutter. Could it, I wonder, be one of those gentleman-burglars of whom I've heard so much? If it really is a burglar, I'd like to see what he looks like.

As far as I can judge, two steps with muddy feet have so far been taken across the kitchen-floor. The third step must have been planted on one of the removable floor-boards for there was a sharp thwacking sound loud enough to echo through the silence of the night. I feel as if the fur on my back were being rubbed in the wrong direction with a boot-brush. For a while there was no further sound, not even the stealthiest footstep. Mrs. Sneaze snores gently on, sucking in and blowing out through her gaping gob the beneficent air of this peaceful era. My master is probably dreaming some dream in which his thumb is trapped in a scarlet book. After a while, there comes the sound of a match being struck in the kitchen. Even a gentleman-thief cannot, as I can, see in the dark. It must be very inconvenient for him.

At this point I crouched well down and tried to work out what moves the intruder would next make. Will he proceed hither from the kitchen by way of the living-room; or will he, turning left through the hall, make his way to the study? I hear the sound of a sliding door, and then footsteps on the veranda. He's gone to the study. Dead silence followed.

It then occurred to me that it would be kind, while there was still time, to wake my master and his wife. But how? A few impractical notions spin round inside my skull like water-wheels, but I am not visited with any sensible ideas. It struck me that I might possibly rouse them by tugging at the bedcovers. Two or three times I tried, worrying away at the lower end of the material, but my efforts had no effect. I then thought I might do better if I rubbed my wet cold nose against my master's cheek. I accordingly put my muzzle to his face, but all I got for my trouble was a sharp smack in the snoot. He didn't even wake but, lifting his arm in his sleep, rapped me hard on the nose. The nose, even in cats, is a vulnerable area and I suffered agonies. Nevertheless I persisted. Since I could think of nothing else, I tried miaowing at them. Indeed I tried. At least twice; but somehow my throat just failed to function and no sound emerged. When at long last and by enormous self-discipline I did manage to emit a single feeble mew, I was quickly shocked back into silence. For, though my master continued just to lie there like a log, suddenly I heard the interloper once more on the move. I hear the little creakings of his inexorable approach along the veranda. This, I think, is it. There's nothing more I can do. So, slipping in between the sliding door and a wickerwork trunk, I get myself into a position suitable at least for this stage of the proceedings: a hidey-hole from which, in the safety of concealment, I can spy upon a criminal at work.

The footsteps advance along the veranda until they are immediately outside the paper-door of my master's bedroom. There they stop dead. I dare not even breathe. My every nerve is at full stretch as I hunch down waiting for the thief's next move. I realized later that my feelings at that time were precisely those which I could expect to feel if I ever hunted rats. It was as though my very soul were about to pounce from my eyes. I am indebted to this thief that, though long ago I resolved never to turn ratter, nevertheless I have been enlightened, this once in my lifetime, as to the nature of the hunting thrill.

The next moment a tiny area in the very middle of the third frame of the paper-door began to change color, to darken as though it had been struck by a raindrop. As I stare at that dampened spot, I can see behind its darkening an object of pale scarlet. Suddenly the paper gives and through it pokes the bare length of a wet red tongue. The tongue seems just to pulse there for a second, and then it vanishes into the darkness. In its place a shining thing, something menacingly glittery, appears in the tongue-licked hole. The eye of a thief. Strangely enough, that gleaming eye seems to disregard all other objects in the room and to be concentrating its gaze directly upon the place where I lurk behind the wickerwork trunk. Though that terrifying inspection cannot have lasted for even so much as a minute, I have never endured a stare so baleful or intense. So to be stared at burns away whole stretches of one's life-expectancy. The scorching of that eye became intolerable, and I had just made up my mind to jump out from behind the trunk when the paper-door slid gently sideways and the thief was at last disclosed to my fascinated sight.

Though at this point it would be normal, in accordance with the established customs of the story-teller's art, to offer a description of this rare and unexpected visitor, I must beg the reader's indulgence for a small digression of which the point and pertinence will, in due course, become clear. My digression takes the form of a statement of my humble views upon the nature of omnipotence and omniscience, both human and divine; views upon which I would invite the discerning comment of all my honored readers.

From time immemorial God has been worshiped as omniscient and omnipotent. In particular, the Christian God, at least up until the twentieth century, was honored for his alleged possession of those qualities. However, that alleged omniscience and omnipotence could well be regarded by the ordinary man in the street as, in fact, their precise opposites: nescience and impotence. I believe that, not since the world was first created, has anyone preceded me in identifying this extraordinary paradox. It is consequently unavoidable that I should feel a certain pride of self-discovery, pride in this revelation that I am indeed no ordinary cat. It is accordingly to drive home to numbskull human beings the unwisdom of sneering at cats that I offer the following analysis of the paradox which, if I had a name, would be named after its inimitable discoverer. I am informed that God created all things in this universe, from which it must follow that God created men. In fact I am advised that this proposition is specifically stated as a fundamental truth in some fat book which human beings call the Bible. Now, mankind has been engaged for several thousands of years in the accumulation of human observations about the facts of humanity. From which mass of data one particular fact has emerged which not only causes human beings to wonder at and admire themselves but also inclines them to acquire ever-deepening credence in the omniscience and omnipotence of God. The particular fact in question is the fact that, although mankind now teems upon this earth, no two human creatures have identical faces. The constituents of the human face are, of course, fixed: two eyes, two ears, a nose and a mouth. Further, the general dimensions of those constituent items are, more or less, the same. Nevertheless, though the myriads of human faces are thus all constructed from the same basic materials, all the final products differ from each other. The human reaction to this state of affairs is not only to rejoice in how bloody marvelous it is that each and every one of them commands an individuality of appearance but also to admire the miraculous skill of the Creator who, using such simple and uniform materials, has yet produced such an infinite variety of result. For surely only a power of infinite originality of imagination could have created such almost incredible diversity. Even the greatest of painters cannot produce, however strenuously he exerts himself in pursuit of variety, more than twelve or thirteen individual master-pieces. So it is natural that mankind should marvel at God's astonishing and single-handed achievement in the production of people. Since such a protean creativity cannot be matched by men as themselves creators, inevitably they regard the process as a mani-festation of divinity and, in particular, of divine omnipotence. For which reasons human beings stand in endless awe of God; and, of course, considered from the human viewpoint, it is entirely understandable that they should.

However, considered from the feline view-point, the same facts lead to the opposite conclusion: that God, if not entirely impo-tent, is at least of limited ability, even incom-petent. Certainly of no greater creative capability than muddle-headed man. God is supposed to have created, of intent, as many faces as there are people. But surely one cannot just dismiss the possibility that, in fact, he lacked sureness of touch; that, though he originally intended to create every man-jack of mankind with the same face, he found the task impossible; and that he consequently produced so long a string of botched appearances as to end up with the present disorderly state of the human physiognomy. Thus the variformity of the human face can equally well be regarded either as a demonstration of God's success or as evidence of his failure. Lacking knowledge of his original creative intent, one can only say that the evidence of the human face argues no more strongly for God's omnipotence than it does for his incompetence.

Consider human eyes. They are embedded in pairs within a flat surface and their owners therefore cannot simultaneously see to both their left and right. It is regrettable, but only one side of any object can, at any one time, enter their field of vision. Being thus incapable of seeing in the round even the daily happenings of life in his own society, it is perhaps not surprising that man should get so excited about certain one-sided aspects of his limited view of reality, and, in particular, should allow himself to fall into awe of God. Any creature capable of seeing things whole must recognize that, if it is difficult to create infinite variation, it is equally difficult to create absolute similitude. Had Raphael ever been asked to paint two absolutely identical portraits of the Madonna, he would have

found it no less irksome than to be pressed
for two pictures of that subject in which
every single detail was totally different.
Indeed, it is probable that the painting of
identical portraits would prove the harder
task. Kōbō Daishi was not only the Great
Teacher but also a master calligrapher. But
had he been asked one morning to inscribe
the two characters of his own name in exactly
the same style as he had done the day before,
he would have found it more difficult than to
write them differently. Consider, too, the
nature of language-learning. Human beings
learn their various tongues purely by imitation. They reproduce, without any display
of initiative or inventiveness, the noises made
by the daily mouthings of their mothers,
nurses and whomsoever else they may happen
to hear. To the best of their ability, they imitate. Nevertheless, in the course of one or two
decades, the languages thus produced by
imitation show distinct changes in pronun-
ciation. Which amply demonstrates the
human inability to make perfect imitations.
Exact imitation is extremely difficult to
achieve. Now if God had shown himself able
to create human beings indistinguishable
from each other, that would have been impressive. If every single one of them appeared
with the self-same features, like so many
mold-cast masks of a fat-faced woman,
then indeed would God's omnipotence have
been tellingly demonstrated. But the actual
state of affairs, a situation in which God has

let loose under the sun all manner of different faces, could well be taken to prove the limited competence of his creative power.

I must confess that I have now forgotten why I embarked upon this digression. However, since similar forgetfulness is common among mankind, I trust such a lapse will be found pardonable in a cat. The fact is that the foregoing thoughts leapt naturally to my mind the moment that the paper-door slid open and I at last clapped eyes upon the thief. Why so? you may ask. Why should the sudden appearance of a thief upon the threshold prompt this closely reasoned, this irrefutable critique of divine omnipotence? As I said, I have forgotten why. But if I may have a moment to recollect my train of thought, I'm sure I can find the reason. Ah yes, I have it.

When I looked at the thief's calm face, I was so struck by one peculiarity that my long-held theories about God's incompetence as a face-creator seemed in that instant to be crumbling down to nothing. For the peculiarity was that the thief's face was the spitting image of the handsome face of our much-loved Avalon Coldmoon. Naturally, I lack acquaintances among the burglaring fraternity: but, basing my judgment on their outrageous behaviors, I had formed my own private picture of a burglar's face. But the face of this particular burglar did not match my image. I had always assumed that a burglar's nostrils would be widely splayed to left and right, that his eyes would be as big and round as copper coins, and that his hair would be close-cropped. But there's a vast difference between the fancied and the fact, so vast one should always be wary of giving free rein to one's imagination. This thief is tall and slimly built, with a charmingly dark-ish complexion and straight, level eyebrows: altogether a very modish sort of burglar. He seems, again like Coldmoon, to be about twenty-six or twenty-seven. Indeed a God so deft as to be able to produce this startling likeness cannot possibly be regarded as in-competent. To tell the truth, the resemblance is so close that my immediate and astonished reaction was to wonder whether, bursting in like this in the middle of the night, Coldmoon had gone mad. It was only when I noticed the absence of any sign of a budding moustache that I realized that the intruder could not possibly be Coldmoon.

Coldmoon is both masculine and hand-some. He has been manufactured by God with such especial care that it is proper he should so easily besot that walking credit-card, Miss Opula Goldfield. Yet, to judge from his appearance, this thief's power to attract women can be no less strong than Coldmoon's. If that Goldfield girl is besotted by Coldmoon's eyes and mouth, it would be no more than a matter of courtesy that she should go into similarly ardent raptures over those of this burglar. Quite apart from the question of courtesy, it would be contrary to logic if she failed to love him. Being so naturally quick-minded and intelligent, she would, of course, immediately grasp the point; and it would follow that, if she were offered the burglar as a substitute for Coldmoon, she would, body and soul, adore him and live with him in conjugal felicity till death did them part. Even if Coldmoon so succumbs to the wiles of Waverhouse that this very rare and excellent match is broken off, still, so long as the burglar remains alive and well, there is no real cause for concern. Having thus projected the possible train of future events, I felt, purely for Miss Goldfield's sake, relieved and reassured. That this noble burglar exists as a husband-in-reserve is, I think, likely to be important to her happiness in life.

The thief is carrying something under his arm. Peering, I discover that it's that decrepit blanket which, a little earlier on, my master had pitched away into his study. The thief is dressed in a short coat of cotton drawn tight below his bottom with a sash of blue-gray silk. His pallid legs are bare from the knees down. Gently he extends one foot from the veranda and sets it softly on the bedroom matting. At which moment my dozing master, no doubt still dreaming that his finger is being savaged by a scarlet book, turns over in his sleep and, as he slumps with a heavy thud into a new position, suddenly shouts "It's Coldmoon!" The burglar drops the blanket and whips back as though he'd trodden on a

scorpion. Through the flimsy paper of the
sliding door, I see the silhouette of two long
legs a-tremble. My master grunts in his
sleep, mumbles something meaningless and
knocks his red book sideways. He then begins
a noisy scratching of his dark-skinned arm as
though he'd caught the scurvy. He suddenly
goes quiet, and lies there fast asleep with his
head off the pillow. His shout of Coldmoon-
recognition relates, not to reality, but to some
incident of dream. Nevertheless for quite a
little while the burglar stood silent on the
veranda watching the room for any further
liveliness. Satisfied at last that my master and
his wife are safely deep in sleep, he re-intrudes
one cautious foot. There is, this time, no
commentary on Coldmoon. Almost at once
the second foot appears.

The glow of the night-lamp which hitherto
had bathed the whole of this six-mat bedroom
is now sharply segmented by the shadow of
the thief. An utter darkness has fallen upon
the wickerwork trunk and reaches halfway up
the wall behind it. I turn my head and see the
shadow of the intruder's skull drifting about
the wall some two-thirds of the way up to the
ceiling. Though the man is certainly handsome, the misshapen shadow of his head, like
some deformed potato, is positively ludicrous.
For a while he stood there staring down at
Mrs. Sneaze's face and then, suddenly and for
goodness knows what reason, broke into a
grin. I was surprised to find that even in such
aimless grinning he was a twin to Coldmoon.

Lying close to Mrs. Sneaze's pillow there is an oblong box, perhaps fifteen inches long and some four inches broad. The lid is nailed down fast and the box itself so placed as to suggest that its contents must be precious. It is in fact that box of yams which, just the other day, Mr. Tatara Sampei presented to the Sneazes on his return from holiday at his family's country place in Karatsu. It is, one must admit, rather unusual to go to sleep with yams to decorate one's bedside; but Mrs. Sneaze is a lady little troubled by notions of propriety of placement. She keeps high-quality cooking-sugar in her chest of drawers, so the presence in her bedroom of pickles, let alone of yams, would hardly even ruffle her placid unconcern. But the burglar, a non-participant in the alleged omniscience of God, could hardly be expected to have such knowledge of her nature and it is consequently understandable that he should jump to the conclusion that a box so carefully kept within hand's reach of a sleeping woman is certain to be worth removing. He lifts and hefts the box. Finding its weight matches his expectations, he nods in satisfaction. It suddenly struck me as extremely funny that this gentleman-thief, this very prepossessing burglar, was about to waste his expert skills in vegetable furacity. However since it could be dangerous to make my presence heard, I hold back the laughter bursting to escape.

The burglar wraps the yam-box carefully in the blanket and looks round the room for

something with which to tie the bundle. His
eye lights upon the sash which my master
threw down on the floor when he was un-
dressing for bed. The burglar ties and knots
the sash around the yam-box and hoists it
smoothly onto his back. I doubt if women
would be attracted to the figure he now presents. He proceeds to stuff two of the children's sleeveless jackets into my master's
knitted underpants. Each of the leg-parts
looks like a snake that has swallowed a frog.
Perhaps their swollen ugliness could be better
compared to the shape of some pregnant
serpent. At all events the shape produced was
odd and rather ugly. If you don't believe me,
try it for yourself. The thief then tied the
pant-legs round his neck, leaving his hands
free for further rummage. Wondering what
he'll nobble next, I watch him closely. He
spreads out my master's silk kimono on the
floor and neatly, quickly, piles upon it Mrs.
Sneaze's *obi,* my master's *haori* and his remaining underwear together with various bits
and bobs which he finds about the room. I
am deeply impressed by the sheer profes-
sionalism of his larceny, the technical polish
of his packaging and parcel-work. First he
fashions a long silk cord by knotting Mrs.
Sneaze's *obi*-string to her waistband-fastener.
With this cord he ties his loot into a tidy
package, and lifts the lot with one hand.
Taking a last look round, he spots a packet of
cheap gaspers lying beside my master's head.
He shoves the packet into his sleeve but, on

second thought, takes it out again and, carefully selecting a cigarette, bends to light it at the flame of the night-lamp. He inhales deeply, like a man content with a job well done. Before the exhaled smoke had thinned to nothingness around the milky glass of the night-lamp's chimney the sound of the burglar's footfalls had faded away into silent distance. Husband and wife remain deep-sunk in slumber. Contrary even to their own idea of themselves, human beings are a careless and unwary lot. I myself feel quite worn out by the night's excitements and, if I now continue this account of them, I shall have some kind of break-down. . . .

I slept both deep and late, so that, when I finally awoke, the sun was already bright in the blue spring sky. My master and his wife were talking to a policeman at the kitchen entrance.

"I see. You reckon he entered here and then worked round toward the bedroom? And you two were asleep and noticed nothing at all?"

"That's right." My master seems a bit embarrassed.

"And about what time did this burglary take place?" The policeman asks the usual silly question. If one could be in a position to state the hour of such an offense, the chances are that no offense would have occurred.

My master and his wife seem not to realize this point and take the question in real earnest.

"I wonder whenabouts it was."

"Well now, let me think," says Mrs. Sneaze. She seems to imagine that by taking thought one can fix the time of events that took place when one was unconscious. "What was the time," she asks her husband, "when you went to bed?"

"It was after you that I went to bed."

"Yes," she agrees, "I went to bed before you did."

"I wonder what time I woke up."

"I think it was at half past seven."

"So what time would that make it when the thief broke in?"

"It must, I suppose, have been sometime in the dead of night."

"Of course it was sometime in the dead of night. But what I'm asking you about is the particular time."

"Well, that I can't just say for certain. Not till I've had a good think." She's still committed to her thinking ways.

The policeman had only asked his potty question as a matter of form, and he is in fact totally indifferent as to the precise time at which the burglar broke in. All he wants is that my master and his wife should give some kind of an answer: any answer, never mind whether true or not, would do. But the victims engage in such pointless and protracted dialogue that the policeman shows signs of irritation. Eventually he snaps at them. "Right then. So the time of the burglary is not known. Is that correct?"

"I suppose it does come down to that," my master answers in his usual drily pedagogic manner.

The policeman was not amused. He plodded stolidly on in accordance with his own routine of police procedure.

"In that case you should send in a written statement of complaint to the effect that on such and such a date in this the thirty-eighth year of the Meiji Era, you, having fastened the entrances to your dwelling, retired to bed; and that subsequently a burglar, having removed such and such a sliding wooden shutter, sneaked into such and such a room or rooms and there stole such and such items of property. Remember, this paper is not just a statement of lost goods but constitutes a formal complaint which may later be used as an accusation. You'd be advised not to address it to anyone in particular."

"Do we have to identify every single item that's been stolen?"

"Yes. Set it all out in a detailed list. Coats, for instance: set down how many have gone, and the value of each one taken. No," he went on in answer to my master's next suggestion, "I don't think it would help much if I stepped inside. The burglary has already taken place." With which unhelpful comment he took himself off.

My master, having planted himself with his writing brush and inkstone in the very center of the room, calls his wife to come and sit beside him. Then, almost in belligerence, he announces "I shall now compose a written statement of complaint. Tell me what's been stolen. Item by item. Sharp, if you please."

"What cheek! Who d'you think you're telling to look sharp? If you talk to me in that dictatorial manner, I shall tell you nothing." Her toilet incomplete, she plonks herself down sulkily beside him.

"Just look at yourself! You might be some cheap tart at a post-town inn. Why aren't you wearing an *obi*?"

"If you don't like how I look, buy me decent clothes. A post-town tart, indeed! How can I dress correctly when half my stuff's been stolen?"

"He took your *obi*? What a despicable thing to do! All right then, we'll start with that. What kind of *obi* was it?"

"What d'you mean? What kind? How many *obi* do you think I've got? It was my black satin with the crêpe lining."

"One *obi* of black satin lined with crêpe . . . And what would you say it cost?"

"About six yen, I think."

"Six yen! That's far too expensive. You know we can't afford to fling our money about on fripperies. Don't spend more than one yen fifty sen on the replacement."

"And where do you think you'd find a decent *obi* at that price? As I always say, you're totally heartless. You couldn't care less how wretchedly your wife may be dressed so long as you yourself look reasonably turned out."

"All right. We'll drop the matter. Now, what's next?"

"A surcoat woven with thrown silk. It was given me as a keepsake of Aunt Kōno. You won't find surcoats these days of that quality."

"I didn't ask for a lecture on the decline of textiles. What would it cost?"

"Not less than fifteen yen."

"You mean you've been going around in a surcoat worth not less than fifteen yen? That's real extravagance. A standard of living miles beyond our means."

"Oh, what does it matter? You didn't even buy it."

"What's the next item?"

"One pair of black foot-gloves."

"Yours?"

"Don't be silly. Whoever heard of a woman wearing black ones? They're yours, of course. And the price, twenty-seven sen."

"Next?"

"One box of yams."

"Did he even filch the yams? I wonder how he'll eat them. Stewed, d'you think? Or in some kind of soup?"

"How the devil should I know? You'd better run along and ask him."

"What were they worth?"

"I wouldn't know the price of yams."

"In that case, let's say twelve yen fifty sen."

"That's ridiculous. How could a box of yams, even ones grown down in Kyushu and then transported here, cost as much as that?"

"You said you didn't know what they would cost."

"I did, and I don't. But twelve fifty would be plain absurd. Far, far too much."

"How can you say in one and the same breath that you don't know their price but that twelve fifty is absurd? It makes no sense at all. Except to prove that you're an Otanchin Palaeologus."

"That I'm a what?"

"That you're an Otanchin Palaeologus."

"What's that?"

One can hardly blame the lady. Though long experience has given me a certain facility in decoding my master's thoughts as expressed in vile puns and twisted references to Japanese provincial slang and the mustier tracts of Western scholarship, this particular demonstration of his skills is both sillier and more obscure than usual. I'm still not sure that I understand his full intention, but I suspect he meant no more than that he thought his wife a blockhead. Why then didn't he just leave it at "Otanchin"? Because, despite his temerarious attack on her balding pate, he lacks the guts to risk a head-on clash and he's not entirely certain that she's never heard that slang-term for a fool. So what does he do? He sees a similarity of sound between "Otanchin" and "Konstantin," the name of the last Palaeologue Emperor of Byzantium. Not that the sounds are sufficiently similar to justify a pun. Not that Constantine the Eleventh has any remote connection with the price of yams.

Not that such truths would sway my master. He simply wants to call his wife a blockhead without having to cope with the consequences of doing so. No wonder Mrs. Sneaze is foxed and no wonder she presses for an explanation.

"Never mind about that. What's next on the list? You haven't yet mentioned my own kimono."

"Never mind about what's next. Just tell me what 'Otanchin Palaeologus' means."

"It hasn't got any meaning."

"You're so excessively clever that I'm sure you could explain what it means if you wanted to. What kind of a fool do you take me for? I bet you've just been calling me names by taking advantage of the fact that I can't speak English."

"Stop talking nonsense and get on with the rest of the list. If we aren't quick in lodging this complaint, we'll never get our property returned."

"It's already too late to make an effective complaint. I'd rather you told me something more about Otanchin Palaeologus."

"You really are making a nuisance of yourself. As I said before, it has no meaning whatever. There's nothing more to be said."

"Well, if that's how you feel, I've nothing more to say about the list."

"What pigheadedness! Have it your own way. I won't then write out this complaint for you."

"Suit yourself. But don't come bothering

me for details of what's missing. It's you, not me, who's lodging the complaint. I just don't care two hoots whether you write it or you don't."

"Then let's forget it," snaps my master. In his usual abrupt manner he gets up and stalks off into his study. Mrs. Sneaze retires to the living-room and dumps herself down in front of her sewing-box. For some ten minutes, this precious pair sit glaring in silence at the paper-door between them.

That was the situation when Mr. Tatara Sampei, donor of yams, came bustling gaily in through the front door. This Tatara was once the Sneazes' houseboy but nowadays, having got his degree in law, he works in the mining department of some big company or other. Like, but junior to, the slippery Suzuki, he's another budding businessman. Nevertheless, because of his former connection with the family, he still occasionally visits the humble dwelling of his erstwhile benefactor. Indeed, having once been almost one of that family, he sometimes spends whole Sundays in the house.

"What wonderful weather, Mrs. Sneaze." He sits on the floor in front of her, with his trousered knees drawn up, and speaks as ever in his own Karatsu dialect.

"Why, hello, Mr. Tatara."

"Is the master out?"

"No, he's in the study."

"It's bad for the health to study as hard as he does. Today's a Sunday; and Sundays don't come every day of the week. Now do they?"

"There's no point in telling me. Go and say it to my husband."

"Yes, but . . ." He looks around the room and then half-asks his hostess "The girls, now, they're not in?" But the words are hardly out of his mouth when Tonko and Sunko both run in from the next room.

"Mr. Tatara, have you brought the goodies?" Tonko, the elder daughter, wastes no time in reminding him of a recent promise.

Tatara scratches his head. "What a memory you've got! I'm sorry I forgot them; but really, next time, I promise to remember."

"What a shame," says Tonko, and her younger sister immediately echoes "What a shame." Mrs. Sneaze, in a modest revival of her natural good humor, smiles slightly.

"I confess I forgot the raw fish goodies, but I did bring round some yams. Have you two girls yet tried them?"

"What's a yam?" asks Tonko; and little Miss Echo pipes up with "What's a yam?"

"Ah, so you've not yet eaten them. Ask your mother to cook you some at once. Karatsu yams are especially delicious, quite different from those you get in Tokyo." As Tatara tootles away on his provincial trumpet, Mrs. Sneaze remembers to thank him again for his kindness.

"It really was kind of you, Mr. Tatara, to bring us yams the other day. And so many of them. Such a generous thought."

"Well, have you eaten them? I had the box made specially so that they wouldn't get broken. I hope you found them undamaged and in their full length."

"I'm sure we would have. But I'm sorry to say that, only last night, the whole lot were stolen by a burglar."

"You've been burgled for yams? What a peculiar criminal. I'd never have dreamt that the passion for yams, even Karatsu yams, could be carried so far." Tatara is enormously impressed.

"Mother," says Tonko, "was there a burglar here last night?"

"Yes," Mrs. Sneaze answers lightly.

"A burglar? Here? A real, real burglar?" Sunko voices wonderment, but immediately goes on to ask "What sort of face did he have?"

Mrs. Sneaze, stumped by this curious question, finds something suitable to say. "He had," she says, looking over at Tatara for sympathetic understanding, "a most fearsome face."

"Do you mean," asks the tactless Tonko, "that he looked like Mr. Tatara?"

"Really, Tonko, that's very rude of you."

"Dear oh dear," laughs the visitor, "is my face as fearsome as all that?" He once more scratches his head. There's a bald patch, about an inch across, on the back of his noddle. It began to appear not much more than a month ago and, though he's taken it round to the quack, it shows no sign of improvement. It is, of course, Tonko who draws attention to the patch.

"Why look," she says, "Mr. Tatara's head is shiny just like mother's."

"Tonko, behave yourself. I told you to be quiet."

"Was the thief's head shiny too?" Sunko innocently asks. In spite of themselves, the adults burst out laughing. Still, the children's chatter so interrupts all conversation that Mrs. Sneaze decides to pack them off. "Run along now and play in the garden. Be good girls and later on I'll find you both some sweeties."

After the girls had gone, Mrs. Sneaze turned to Tatara and with all the gravity of a fellow sufferer enquired "Mr. Tatara, what has happened to your head?"

"Some kind of skin-infection. Not exactly moth, but a bug of some sort which takes ages to clear up. Are you having the same trouble?"

"Ugh! don't talk about bugs. In my case the trouble's the usual female problem of the hair thinning because it's drawn so tight in the married woman's hair-style."

"All baldness is caused by bacteria."

"Well, mine's not."

"Come, come, Mrs. Sneaze, you're being obstinate. One cannot fly in the face of the scientific facts."

"Say what you like, it's not bacteria. But tell me, what's the English word for baldness?"

Tatara said he wasn't sure, but he answered her correctly.

"No, no," she said, "Not that, it's a very much longer word."

"Why not ask your husband? He could tell you straight off."

"I'm asking you precisely because he refuses to help."

"Well, all I know is 'baldness.' You say the word you want's much longer. Can you give me an idea of its sound?"

" 'Otanchin Palaeologus.' I have an idea that 'Otanchin' means bald and 'Palaeologus' head."

"Possibly. I'll pop into the master's study a little later and look it up for you in Webster's dictionary. By the way, the master is eccentric, isn't he? Fancy staying indoors and doing nothing on such a lovely day! No wonder his stomach-troubles never get better. Why don't you persuade him to go and view the flowers at Ueno?"

"Please, you ask him. He never listens to what a woman says."

"Is he still licking jam?"

"Yes, as always."

"The other day he was complaining that you're always telling him he overdoes it. 'But she's wrong,' he said, 'I really don't eat all that much.' So I told him the obvious answer was that you and the girls are also fond of jam. . . ."

"Mr. Tatara, how could you say such a thing!"

"But, Mrs. Sneaze, you've got a jam-licker's face."

"How can you tell a thing like that by looking at someone's face?"

"I can't, of course. But, honestly, Mrs. Sneaze, don't you ever take any?"

"Well, naturally I sometimes take a little. And why shouldn't I? After all, it's ours."

Tatara laughed right out. "I thought that was the answer. But seriously," he said, adopting a more sober tone, "that really was bad luck about the burglar. Was it only yams that he filched?"

"If it were only yams, we wouldn't be so upset. But he's taken all our everyday clothing."

"Then you really are in trouble. Will you have to borrow money again? If only this thing here were a dog, not just an idle cat. . . . What a difference that might have made. Honestly, you ought to keep a dog, a big sturdy dog. Cats are practically useless. All they do is eat. This cat, for instance; has it ever even caught a rat?"

"Not a single one. It's a very lazy and impudent cat."

"Ah! that's terrible. You must get rid of it at once. Shall I take it along with me? Boiled, you know, they're really quite good eating."

"Don't tell me you eat cats!"

"Yes, indeed, every now and again. They taste delicious."

"You must have a remarkably strong stomach."

I have heard that among these degraded houseboys there are some so close to outright barbarism that they do, in fact, eat cats: but not until now had I ever dreamt that our Tatara, a person with whom I'd long been on terms of quite some coziness, could be so base a creature. Of course he's not our houseboy any longer. Far from it. Though barely out of university, he is now not only a distinguished Bachelor of Law but also a rising executive in that well-known limited company, Mutsui Products. I was therefore more than surprised. The proverb says "When you see a man, take him for a felon"; and the truth of that adage has been well demonstrated by the thieving conduct of last night's pseudo-Coldmoon. Thanks now to Tatara, I have just invented another proverb: "When you see a man, take him for a felophage." The longer one lives in this wicked world, the more one learns. It is always good to learn; but as one accumulates knowledge of the world's wickedness, one grows ever the more cautious, ever the more prepared for the worst. Artfulness, uncharitableness, self-defensive wariness: these are the fruits of worldly learning. The penalty of age is this rather ugly knowingness. Which would seem to explain why one never finds among the old a single decent person. They know too much to see things straight, to feel things cleanly, to act without compromise.

Thinking that there might then be some merit in departing this world while still in my prime, I was making myself small in a corner lest such a departure should be forced upon me in the company of onions stewing in Tatara's pot, when my master, drawn from his study by the sound of Tatara's voice, slouched back into the living room.

"I hear, sir, you've been burgled. What a stupid thing to have happen." Tatara opens the conversation somewhat bluntly.

"That yam-purloiner was certainly stupid." My master has no doubt whatever of his own profound intelligence.

"Indeed the thief was stupid: but his victim wasn't exactly clever."

"Perhaps those with nothing worth stealing, people like Mr. Tatara, are the cleverest of all." Rather surprisingly Mrs. Sneaze comes out on her husband's side.

"Anyway, one thing's clear. That this cat's totally useless. Really, one can't imagine what it thinks it's for. It catches no rats. It sits calmly by while a burglar breaks in. It serves no purpose whatsoever. How about letting me take it off?"

"Well," says my master, "maybe I will. What would you do with it?"

"Cook it and eat it."

On hearing that ferocious proposition, my master gave vent to a sinister wail of dyspeptic laughter but he answered neither yes nor no. This, to my mingled surprise and glad relief, seemed to satisfy Tatara for he pressed no further with his disgusting proposal. After a brief pause, my master, changing the subject, remarks "The cat doesn't matter but I do object most strongly to anyone stealing my clothes. I feel so cold." He looks indeed dispirited; and no wonder he feels cold. Until yesterday he was wearing two quilted kimonos: but today, wearing only a single lined-kimono and a short-sleeved shirt, he's been sitting about since morning and has taken no exercise. What little blood he has is totally engaged in keeping his miserable stomach going, so naturally it doesn't get round to his arms and legs.

"It's hopeless being a teacher. Your world gets turned upside down by a mere burglar. It's still not too late to make a change. Why not come into the business world?"

"Since my scholarly spouse just doesn't care for businessmen, it's a waste of time even to suggest the idea." Mrs. Sneaze, of course, would be delighted to see him go into business.

"How many years is it," Tatara asks, "since you took your degree?"

"Eight years, I think," answers Mrs. Sneaze looking toward her husband. My master neither confirms nor denies the period.

"Eight years and your pay's the same as on the day you started. However hard you study, no one appreciates your merits. 'All by himself the master is, and lonely.' " For Mrs. Sneaze's benefit Tatara quotes a scrap of Chinese poetry remembered from his days in middle school. Since she fails to understand him she makes no answer.

"Of course I don't like teaching, but I dislike commerce even more." My master seems to be a bit uncertain in his own mind what it is he does like.

"He dislikes everything," says Mrs. Sneaze.

"Well, anyway I'm sure he doesn't dislike his wife." Tatara makes an unexpected sally.

"I dislike her most of all." My master's comment is extremely terse.

Mrs. Sneaze turns slightly away and her face stiffens, but she then looks back at her husband and says, as if she thought she were getting a good dig in at him, "I suppose you'll be saying next that you dislike living."

"True," came his off-hand answer, taking the wind clean out of her sails, "I don't like living much." He's way past praying for.

"You should go for a brisk walk every now and again. Staying indoors all day must be ruining your health. And what's more, you really should become a businessman. Making money is simple as pie."

"Look who's talking. You yourself aren't exactly rolling in it."

"Ah, well. But I only joined the company last year. Even so, I've more saved up than you have."

"How much have you saved?" Inevitably Mrs. Sneaze rises to such bait, and puts her question with real earnestness.

"Fifty yen, already."

"And how much is your salary?" Again it's Mrs. Sneaze who asks the question.

"Thirty yen a month. The company retains

five yen and saves it up for me. In an emergency I can draw on the accumulated capital. Really, why don't you buy some tramway shares with your pin-money? Their value will double within three or four months. Indeed anyone with a bit of capital could double, even treble, his money in next to no time."

"If I had any pin-money," Mrs. Sneaze somewhat sourly observes, "I wouldn't now be up a gum-tree all on account of some petty theft."

"That's why I keep saying your husband should go into business. For instance, if he'd studied law and then joined a company or a bank, he would by now be earning three or four hundred yen a month. It seems a shame he didn't. By the way, sir, do you happen to know a man called Suzuki Tōjūrō who got his degree in engineering?"

"Yes, he called here only yesterday."

"So you've seen him then. I ran into him a few days back at a party and your name cropped up. I said I'd once been a member of your household and he replied that he and you had once shared lodgings at some temple in Koishikawa. 'Next time you see him,' he said, 'please give him my kindest regards and say I'll be looking him up one of these days.'"

"I gather he's recently been transferred back to Tokyo."

"That's right. Until the other day he was pining away somewhere down in Kyushu but he's just been moved up to the head office here in Tokyo. He's a smooth lad, that one.

Smooth as a keg of lacquer. He even takes the trouble to speak engagingly to me. . . . Have you any idea how much he earns?"

"Not the foggiest."

"Well, on top of his basic monthly pay of 250 yen, he'll be getting bonuses twice a year, in July and December, so that his overall income can't be less than four or five hundred yen each month. To think that a man like that can be coining the stuff while you, a teacher of the English Reader, can scarcely make ends meet. It's a lunatic state of affairs."

"Lunatic's the word." Even a man as snooty and superior as my master is no different from the herd of his fellow-men when it comes to matters of money. Indeed, the very fact that he's skint the whole year long makes him rather more keen than most to get his claws on a copper. However, having spoken at such length on the marvels of making money, Tatara has now exhausted his stock of slogans about the beatitudes of the business life: so he turns to Mrs. Sneaze on a totally different tack.

"Does a man called Coldmoon come visiting your husband?"

"Yes, often."

"What sort of fellow is he?"

"I'm told he's a brilliant scholar."

"Handsome, would you say?"

Mrs. Sneaze permits herself an unbecoming titter. "I'd say that in looks he's just about as good-looking as you."

"How do you come to be interested in
Coldmoon?" enquires my master.

"The other day someone asked me to ask
around about him. Is he a man worth making
enquiries about?" Even before he gets an
answer, Tatara shows by his condescending
tone that he doesn't think much of Coldmoon.

"As a man," says my master, "he's a great
deal more impressive than you."

"Is he, now? More impressive than me?"
Characteristically, Tatara neither smiles nor
seems offended. A sensitive man of the utmost
self-control? A dense unfeeling dullard? Need
one ask? He eats cats, doesn't he? "But tell
me, will this Coldmoon fellow be getting a
doctorate one of these days?"

"I'm told he's writing a thesis now."

"So he's a fool after all. . . . Writing a thesis
for a doctorate indeed! I'd expected him to
be brighter than that."

"You don't half fancy yourself," says Mrs.
Sneaze with a laugh. "You always did reckon
yourself the bee's knees and the cat's whisk-
ers. But what's so foolish about being well
educated?"

"Someone told me that once this Coldmoon gets his doctorate, then he'll be given
someone's daughter. Something like that. So
of course I said 'A man's a fool who works
for a doctorate just to marry a girl. Someone
should not marry someone's daughter to

anyone so foolish. Better far,' I said, 'for someone's daughter to marry me.' "

My master wobbled his head. "To whom did you say all that?"

"To the man who asked me to ask around about Coldmoon."

"Suzuki?"

"Golly, no. I wouldn't be bandying words with a big shot like that on such a delicate matter. At least, not yet I wouldn't."

"A lion at home, a wood-louse in the open!" says Mrs. Sneaze. "You talk big, Mr. Tatara, when you're here with us, but I bet you curl up small and quiet when you talk to Mr. Suzuki."

"Of course I do. It would be foolhardy to do anything else. One word wrong and I could be out on my ear."

"Tatara," my master suddenly breaks in, "let's go out for a walk." Sitting there in the scanty remnants of his wardrobe he's grown to feel downright frozen, and the thought's just filtered through that the exercise of walking might warm him up a bit. There can be no other explanation for such an unprecedented suggestion.

Tatara, that unpetrine person, that seaweed in the tide-flows of the world, that reed which bends to its lightest wind, doesn't even hesitate. "Yes, indeed, let's go. How about Ueno? Let's go try some of Imozaka's famous dumplings. Have you ever tried those dumplings? You, too, Mrs. Sneaze, sometime you really ought, if only just once, to try them.

They're beautifully soft and even more beautifully cheap. They even serve *saké* as well."
Tatara was still babbling away about dumplings when my master, his hat on his head,
was ready on the doorstone waiting to leave.
. . .

Myself, I need rest. There's no conceivable
reason why I should keep watch upon, still
less record, how my master and Tatara behaved at Ueno Park, how many plates of
dumplings they consumed and what other
pointless happenings transpired. In any case
I lack the energy to trail along after them. I
shall therefore skip all mention of their
afternoon doings and, instead, relax. All
created things are entitled to demand of their
Creator some rest for recreation. We are born
with an obligation to keep going while we can
and if, like maggots wriggling in the fabric of
this world, we are to keep on thrashing about
down here, we do need rest to do it. If the
Creator should take the line that I am born to
work and not to sleep, I would agree that I am
indeed born to work but I would also make
the unanswerable point that I cannot work
unless I also rest. Even my master, that timid
but complaining crank in the grinding mecha-
nism of our national education, sometimes,
though it costs him money, takes a weekday
off. I am no human cog. I am a cat, a being
sensitive to the most subtle shades of thought
and feeling. Naturally I tire more quickly
than my master. Naturally I need more
sleep. But I confess I'm a little worried by

Tatara's recent travesty of my case, his wicked misrepresentation of my natural need for sleep as evidence of my practical uselessness. Philistines such as he, creatures responsive only to the crudest material phenomena, cannot appreciate anything deeper than the surface appearances recorded by their five coarse senses. Unless one is rigged out in a navvy's clobber and the sweat can be seen and smelt as it pours from one's brow and armpits, such persons can't conceive that one is working. I have heard there was a Zen priest called, I fancy, Bodhidharma, who remained so long immobilized in spiritual meditation that his legs just rotted away. That he made no move, even when ivies crept through the wall and then spreading suckers sealed his eyes and mouth, did not mean that the priest was sleeping or dead. On the contrary, his mind was very much alive. Legless in the bonds of dusty vegetation, Bodhidharma came to grasp such brilliantly stylish truths as the notion that, since Zen is of itself so vast and so illumining, there can be no appreciable distinction between saints and mediocrities. What's more, I understand that the followers of Confucius also practice forms of meditation though not perhaps to the extent of self-immurement and of training their flesh to crippledom by idleness.

All such meditants have powers burning in the brain that are a lot more fierce than anything non-meditants could possibly conceive. But because the outward appearance of these

spiritual giants is so solemn, calm, unutterably
serene, the fathead nincompoops who come
and stare at them can see nothing more than
ordinary persons in states of coma, catatonia
or even simple syncope. Such mediocrities
slander their betters as drones and layabouts.
But the fault lies in the very ordinariness of
the eyes of ordinary people, for, in truth,
their eyesight is defective in that their glances
merely slither over external appearances,
never pierce through to spiritual inwardness.
Now it is understandable that a man like
Tatara Sampei, that personification of all
things superficial, would only see shit on a
shovel if, undergoing the Zen test of a man's
ability to find purity among impurities, he
were so shown a shitten shovel. But it grieves
me to the core to find that my master who,
after all, has read fairly widely and ought to
be able to see some little way beyond the
mere surface of things, should nevertheless so
readily concur in the flippertigibbet fancies of
his shallow houseboy; at least to the extent of
failing to raise objections to his casserole of
cat.

However, when I think things over and see
them in perspective, I can understand that
it's not altogether unreasonable that my
master and his houseboy should thus look
down on me. Two relevant sayings by ancient
Chinese sages occur to my mind. "Elevated
and noble music cannot penetrate the ears of
the worldly wise" and "Everyone sings
street-songs but very few can join in singing

such learned airs as Shining Spring and White Snow." It's a waste of effort to try and force those incapable of seeing more than outer forms to understand the inner brilliance of their own souls. It is like pressing a shaven priest to do his hair in a bun, like asking a tunny-fish to deliver a lecture, like urging a tram to abandon its rails, like advising my master to change his job, like telling Tatara to think no more about money. In short, it is exorbitant to expect men to be other than they are. Now the cat is a social animal and, as such, however highly he may rate his own true worth, he must contrive to remain, at least to some extent, in harmony with society as a whole. It is indeed a matter for regret that my master and his wife, even such creatures as O-san and Tatara, do not treat me with that degree of respect which I properly deserve; but nothing can be done about it. That's the way things are; and it would be very much worse, indeed fatal, if in their ignorance they went so far as to kill me, flay me, serve up my butchered flesh at Tatara's dinner-table and sell my emptied skin to a maker of cat-banjos. Since I am a truly unusual cat, one born into this world with a mission demanding purely mental activity, I am responsible for safeguarding the inestimable worth of my own rarity. As the proverb says, "The rich man's son is never seated at the edge of the raised hall." I, too, am far too precious to be exposed to the danger of a tumble into calamity. If sheer vainglory led me to run such risks, I would not only be inviting personal disaster but flouting the evident will of Heaven. However, even the fiercest tiger, once installed in a zoo, settles down resignedly next to some filthy pig. Even the largest of wild geese, once in the poulterer's hands, must finish up on the selfsame chopping board as the scrawniest chickling. Consequently, for as long as I consort with ordinary men, I must conduct myself as if I were an ordinary cat. Ordinary cats catch rats. This long but faultless chain of logic leads to but one conclusion. I have finally decided to catch a rat.

I understand that, now for some time, Japan has been at war with Russia. Being a Japanese cat, I naturally side with Japan. I have even been cherishing a vague ambition to organize some kind of Cats Brigade which, if only a scratch formation, could still inflict claw-damage on the Russian horde. Being thus magnificently militant, why should I dither over a miserable rat or two? So long as the will to catch them burns within me, why, I could rake them in with my eyes shut. Long ago, when someone asked a well-known Zen priest of that ancient time how to attain enlightenment, the priest replied "You should proceed like a cat stalking a rat." Indeed, such utter concentration on one's objective is always certain to bring success. There is, of course, that other proverb which warns against over-cleverness. The over-clever woman may well have failed to sell her cow, but I've never heard it suggested that an over-clever cat might fail to catch a rat. Thus a cat of my outstanding qualities should have no trouble in catching any rat around. Indeed, I cannot see how I could fail to catch one. The fact that up till now I've not caught any reflects no more than my erstwhile disinclination to do so. Nothing more than that.

Just as yesterday, the spring sun sets and flurries of falling cherry-blossoms, whirled on occasional gusts of the evening wind, burst in through the broken kitchen-door. Floating on the water in a kitchen-pail, they glimmer whitely in the dim light of a kitchen-lamp. Now that I have decided to surprise the entire household with the feat of arms which I purpose to achieve during the coming night, I realize that some preliminary reconnaissance of the battlefield is needed to ensure my proper grasp of the topography of the ground. The field of maneuver is not particularly large, covering perhaps an area of four mats. Of that area a full eighth is occupied by the sink, while another eighth consists of that unfloored space where roundsmen from the wine-shop and the greengrocer's stand to wait for the day's order. The stove is unexpectedly grand for a poor man's kitchen and it even boasts a brilliantly shiny copper kettle. Behind the stove, on a strip of wooden boarding about two feet wide, stands the abalone-shell in which I am served my meals. Close to the living-room there is a cupboard for plates and bowls which, being six feet long, severely reduces the already limited space. Beside the cupboard and reaching roughly up to the level of its top, shelves extend along the wall; and on one of the lower shelves there is an earthenware mortar with a small pail placed inside it upside down. A wooden pestle and a radish-grater hang side by side from hooks, and ranged beside them there's a dreary-looking pot for extinguishing live charcoal. From the point where the blackened rafters cross, a pot-hook is suspended, and on that hook a large flat basket floats in mid-air. Every now and again, under the pressure of the kitchen's drafts, the basket moves with a certain magnanimity. When I was a newcomer to this house, I simply could not understand why this basket hung where it did; but, learning later that it was so placed specifically to prevent cats getting at the food which it contained, I realized once again how thoroughly mean, how preternaturally bloody-minded, are the hearts and heads of humankind. The reconnaissance completed, one must plan a campaign appropriate to the site. But a battle with rats can only take place where rats are available to be fought. However brilliantly one may position one's forces, they can achieve nothing if they are alone upon the field. It was thus obviously vital to determine where the rats were most likely to appear. Standing in the middle of the kitchen, I look around and wonder from what direction they would probably emerge. I feel as Admiral Tōgō must have done as he pondered the likeliest course of the Russian fleet.

That awful O-san went off to a bathhouse a little while ago and she hasn't yet come back. Long ago the children went to sleep. My master ate dumplings at Imozaka, came home and has now vanished into his study. His wife, I don't know what she's doing but I would guess she's dozing somewhere deep in yammy dreams. An occasional rickshaw can be heard passing along the street in front of the house: each subsequent silence makes the night more deep, its desolation lonelier. My decision to take action, my sense of resolute high spirit, the waiting kitchen-battlefield, the all-pervading feeling of loneliness: it is the perfect setting and atmosphere for deeds of high renown. There's no least doubt about it. I am the Admiral Tōgō of the cats. Anyone so placed must feel, however terrifying the situation, a certain wild exhilaration; but I confess that, underneath that pleasurable excitement, I was persistently nagged by one disquieting consideration. I have decided to do battle with rats, so I care nothing for the mere number of the rats to be fought; but I do find it worryingly inconvenient not to know from which direction or directions the rats will make their appearance. I have collated and analyzed the results of my recent reconnaissance, and have concluded that there are three lines of advance by which these robber riffraff might debouch upon the field. If they

are gutter-rats, they'll come sneaking up the
drainpipe to the sink and thence nip round
behind the stove. In which case, my correct
tactic is to be in hiding behind the charcoal-
extinguisher and thence interdict their line of
retreat. Alternatively, such villains might
slide in through the hole cut at the base of the
washroom's plaster-wall for the escape of
dirty water into the outside drain: if they
adopt that point of entry, they could then
sneak across the washroom and so pop out
into the kitchen. In which case, my best
tactic is to station myself on the lid of the
rice-cooker from which position, as the filthy
brutes glide past below me, I could drop upon
them from the sky. Finally, my visual check of
the terrain has revealed, at the bottom right-
hand corner of the cupboard, a gnawed half-
moon of a hole which looks suspiciously
convenient for raiding rats. Putting my nose
to the place, I sniff the ground. It smells a
little ratty. If a rat comes dashing out to
battle from that curved sally-port, my best
tactic is to lurk behind the pillar and pounce
upon him from the side as he scuttles by.

A further thought then struck me. Suppose
the rats should find some line of advance
along unexpectedly higher ground. I look up
and the soot-black ceiling gleams evilly in the
glow of the lamp. It looks like hell hung
upside down. It is plain that with my limited
strength and skills I could neither climb up
there, still less climb down. Either because if
I can't, rats can't, or because if I can't, rats

wouldn't, I decide that there's no likelihood that they will descend from those infernal altitudes; and I accordingly abandon any attempt to make plans to cope with that threat. Even so, there's danger of being simultaneously attacked from three directions. If they come from only a single direction, with one eye shut I could wipe the whole lot out. If from two directions, still I'd be able to cope. But if they come from three directions, however confident I may be of my instinctive aptitude for catching rats, the situation would be distinctly dicey. It would be an affront to my own dignity to go beg help from such as Rickshaw Blacky. What on earth shall I do? When, having wondered what on earth to do, one still can't think of anything, it is, I've found, the shortest cut to ease of mind to decide that what one fears won't happen. In point of fact, everyone chooses to assume that the insupportable will never occur. Look round at the world. Today's delighted bride holds no guarantee against death tomorrow; but the bridegroom, happily chanting auspicious texts, displays no sign of worry. The fact that he doesn't worry is not because there's nothing to be worried about. The reason is that, however much he worries, it will not make the slightest difference. So, too, in my case. I've no reason whatever to assert that simultaneous triple-pronged attacks will certainly never be launched, but to decide that they won't sorts best with my self-assurance. All things need assurance. Not least myself. I have consequently reached the firm conclusion that attacks from three directions will not happen.

Even so I still feel tweaks of doubt. I pondered the cause of this continuing uneasiness and worried away at the problem till at last I understood the source of my disquiet. It is the agony of not being able to find a single clear-cut answer to a problem: in my case, to the problem of deciding which of three strategies will prove most profitable. If rats emerge from the cupboard, I have a plan to deal with the situation. If they appear from the bathroom, I have another scheme to cope with that. And if they come sneaking up through the sink, I have yet another wheeze worked out to settle their slithery hash. But to choose one of these three courses of action and then stick firmly to my choice, that I find excruciatingly difficult. I hear that Admiral Tōgō was similarly excruciated as he pondered whether the Russian Baltic Fleet would pass through the Straits of Tsushima or would steer a more easterly course for the Straits of Tsugaru or would take the longest way round by heading out into the Pacific and then swinging back through the Straits of La Pérouse between Hokkaido and Sakhalin. My own predicament enabled me fully to appreciate just how worried the noble Admiral must have been. Not only am I placed in a similar situation but I share his agony of choice.

While I was thus absorbed in contriving a

solution to my problem of major strategy, the damaged paper-door was suddenly slid open and the ugly face of O-san loomed into view. I do not intend that turn of phrase to imply that that creature lacks arms and legs; simply that the remainder of her carcass was so indistinguishable from the background darkness that only her face, hectically bright and savagely colored, struck upon my eyes. She has just returned from the public bathhouse, and her normally red cheeks look positively scarlet. Even though it is still quite early, she proceeds, probably in belated wisdom learnt from last night's happenings, carefully to fasten up the kitchen door. From the study comes my master's voice enjoining her to place his walking-stick at hand's reach by his bedside. Really, I fail to see why such a man should want to decorate his bedside with a walking-stick. Can it be that he's started to fancy himself in the role of that heroic assassin who, so the classics tell us, attacked the first of the Chinese Emperors? Can it be that he sees his walking-stick as that tomb-treasure sword which, at a robber's touch, roared like a tiger, growled like a dragon and then flew upward into the sky? Surely not even my mazy master could harbor such daft delusions. But yesterday it was the yams. Now it's a walking-stick. What will it be tomorrow?

The night is still young. The rats are not likely to appear for some time yet. I need repose before the coming battle.

There are no windows in my master's

kitchen. Instead, just below the level of the ceiling there's a sort of transom about one foot wide which, left open all the year round, serves as a skylight. I was brought suddenly out of my sleep by a flurry of blossoms from the early-flowering cherries blown through that opening on a gust of wind. A hazy moonlight slants into the kitchen and casts a shadow of the stove sidelong across the wooden floor. Wondering if I have overslept, I shake my ears two or three times and then look carefully round to see if anything's developed. Dead silence reigns, through which, as was the case last night, the clock ticks steadily on. It's high time that the rats came out. I wonder where they will appear. It's not long before gentle noises start up inside the cupboard. It sounds as though rats are trying to get at something on a plate and are scrabbling at the plate's edge with their horny claws. In the expectation that these cupboard-rats will eventually emerge from the gnawed half-moon at the bottom of its door, I hunker down to wait beside that opening. The rats seem in no hurry to come out. Eventually the plate-noise stopped but was soon succeeded by sounds of rat-feet on some sort of bowl or basin. Every now and again there were heavy bumpings on the other side of the cupboard door, only a bare three inches distant from the tip of my waiting nose. Sometimes the sounds come even closer to the hole, but then they scamper away again and not one single rat so much as shows its face. Just beyond that door the foe is rampaging through the cupboard, but all I can do is lurk here quietly at the half-moon exit. Which calls for patience; very great patience. The rats, like the Russians in the basin of Port Arthur, seem to be having a rare old shindig in their bowl. I wish that that fool O-san had had the nous to leave the cupboard-door at least sufficiently ajar to allow me to slip through; but what can one expect from so thick-skulled a country bumpkin.

From behind the stove my abalone-shell emits a sound of gentle rocking. Aha! The enemy is also coming from that direction. Very well then. I creep forward on the stealthiest of paws but catch only a glimpse of a tail among the buckets before it whisks away below the sink. A short while later I hear the clink of my master's gargling-glass against the metal of the wash-basin. So! Now they are behind me. As I turn to face this new danger, a whopping great rat, at least six inches long, adroitly tips a small bag of tooth-powder off the shelf above the basin and then itself goes skittering away to safety under the floorboards. Determined not to let him escape, I spring down after him: but even before I'd landed, the filthy beast had vanished. Catching rats, I find, is more tricky than I'd thought. Perhaps I am congenitally incapable of catching them.

When I advance upon the bathroom, rats pop out of the cupboard. When I take post by

the cupboard, rats erupt from the sink. And
when I plant myself firmly in the center of the
kitchen, rats shoot racketing up on all three
fronts together. Never have I seen such impudent bravado combined with such pol-
troonery! Their skittering evasion of fair
fight brands them unworthy adversaries for a
gentleman. Fifteen, maybe sixteen times I
darted hither and thither until, all to no
purpose, I had exhausted myself both phys-
ically and mentally. I am ashamed to confess
my failure, but against such mean-souled
adversaries even the resourceful Admiral
Tōgō would have found himself stumped. I
had launched upon this venture with high
courage, a determination to subdue the foe,
and even a certain elevated sense of the spiritual beauty of my undertaking: but now,
fagged out and downright sleepy, I find it
merely fatuous and irksome. I cease to rush
around and squat down right in the center of
the kitchen. But, though utterly motionless, if
I maintain a sharp lookout all round me, the
enemy, being such miserable dastards, will
never dare to try on anything serious. When,
unexpectedly, one's enemy turns out to be so
pettily paltry, the sense of war as an honorable
activity cannot be sustained and one is left
with nothing but a feeling of naked hatred.
When that acrid animosity dulls, one becomes downhearted and even absent-minded.
And after that general dimness fades away,
one just feels sleepy. So deep is the lethargy of
complete disdain that one feels prepared to

let one's foes do anything they like. For what of any possible significance, so one asks oneself, are beings so debased capable of doing? Having myself gone through all those stages, I too eventually grew sleepy. And dozed off. All that lives must rest, even in the midst of enemies.

I woke to find a violent wind blowing around me. Again a gust was pitching handfuls of petals through the open transom running along below the eaves. At the very moment of my waking, something, shooting out from the cupboard like a bullet from a gun, sliced across the blowing wind and, quick as a flash, fastened its snapping teeth into my left ear. I'd barely time to realize what was happening before another black shadow flickered round behind me and closed its jaws upon my tail. This all took place within the batting of an eye. Taking no thought whatever, by simple reflex action I spring to my feet. Converting all my strength into a shuddering paroxysm of my skin, I try to shake these monsters off. The demon anchored to my ear, yanked off his feet as I sprang to mine, dangles down beside my face. The end of his tail, spongily soft like a rubber tube, falls unexpectedly into my mouth. I take a firm grip on the beastly object and, teeth clamped fast upon it, I waggle my head from side to side as hard as I can go. The tail came off in my jaws, while the jactitated body, slung first against the wall plastered with old newspapers, bounced off onto the floor-

boards. While the rat still struggles to regain
his balance, quick to seize my chance I pounce
upon him: but, like some rebounding ball, he
whizzes up past my descending muzzle and
lands suprisingly high on one of the upper
shelves. Tucking in his legs, he stares down at
me over the edge of his shelf. I stare up at him
from the wooden floor. The distance between
us is about five feet. Clean across that distance
the moonlight slants from the transom like a
woman's broad white sash stretched out along
the air.

Concentrating all my strength in my legs, I
leapt up at the shelf. My front paws grasp its
edge but, weighted down by the rat still
riveted to my tail, my hindlegs are left
scrabbling in mid-air. I am in danger. I try to
clamber upward by judicious adjustment of
the positions of my paws, but each such
effort, by reason of the rat-weight on my
tail, merely results in a weakening of my
pawhold. If my paws slip just one further
quarter of an inch I shall be lost. I am really
in great danger. My claws scrape noisily along
the wooden ledge. In a last effort I try to
advance my left paw, but its claws fail to gain
purchase in the smooth wood surface and I
finish up hanging by a single claw of my right
paw. My body, dragged fully out under its
own and the rear rat's weight, begins both to
swing and to rotate. The monster on the
shelf, which has hitherto been content to sit
motionless and glare at me, now hops down
onto my forehead. My last claw loses hold.

Melded into one black lump, the three bodies plummet downward through the slanted moonlight. Objects on the shelf below, the earthenware mortar, the small pail standing inside it and an empty tin, swell the falling lump which, further swollen by the dislodgement of a charcoal extinguisher, finally splits in two. Half the ugly mass falls straight into a water-jar while the rest disintegrates into bodies wildly rolling across the kitchen floor. In the dead quiet of middlenight the noise was truly appalling. Even my own already frantic soul was further shaken by the din.

"Burglars!" Hoarsely bellowing, my master comes rushing out from the bedroom. He carries a lamp in one hand and a walking-stick in the other. From his sleepy eyes there flashes as much of the light of battle as such a man could be expected ever to muster. I crouch down silently beside my abalone-shell. The two rat-monsters vanish into the cupboard. "What's going on here? Who made all that hideous noise?" My master, looking vaguely sheepish, shouts in his angriest voice questions that no one's there to answer.

The westering moon sank steadily lower and lower, and its broad white sash of light across the kitchen narrowed and narrowed as it sank.

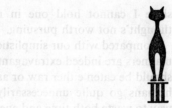

THIS HEAT is quite unbearable, especially for a cat. An English clergyman, a certain Sydney Smith, once remarked that the weather was so intolerably hot that there was nothing left for it but to take off his skin and sit about in his bones. Though to be reduced to a skeleton might be going too far, I would at least be glad to slip out of my fur of spotted palish gray and send it to be washed or even popped temporarily into pawn. To human eyes, the feline way of life may seem both extremely simple and extremely inexpensive, for cats' faces look the same all the year round and we wear the same old only suit through each of the four seasons. But cats, I can assure you, just like anyone else, feel the heat and feel the cold. There are times when I consider that I really wouldn't mind, just that once, soaking myself in a bath: but if I got hot water all over my fur, it would take ages to get dry again and that is why I grin and bear the stink of my own sweat and have never in all my life yet passed through the entrance of a public bathhouse. Every now and again I think about using a fan but, 133 since I cannot hold one in my paws, the thought's not worth pursuing.

Compared with our simplistic style, human manners are indeed extravagant. Some things should be eaten either raw or as they are: but humans go quite unnecessarily out of their way to waste both time and energy on boiling them, grilling them, pickling them in vinegar and smarming them over with bean-paste. The horrible results of all these processes appear to tickle them to death. In matters of dress they are similarly absurd. Inasmuch as they are born imperfect, it might be asking too much if one expected them to wear, as is the custom of cats, the same clothes all year long but, surely to goodness, they cannot need to swaddle their skins in such a heterogeneity of sheer clobber. Since it seems not to shame them to be indebted to sheep, to be dependent on silkworms and even to accept the charity of cotton-shrubs, one could almost assert that their extravagance is an admission of incompetence.

Even if one overlooks their oddity and allows them their perversities in matters of food and clothing, I completely fail to see why they have to exhibit this same crass idiosyncrasy in matters that have no bearing whatsoever on their continuing existence. Take, for instance, their hair. Since, willynilly, it grows, I would have thought it simplest and best for any creature just to leave it alone. But no. Not for humans. Totally unnecessarily, they trick themselves out in every conceivable sort and kind of hair-do. And even take pride in their idiot variations. Those who call themselves priests keep their heads clean-shaven blue: blue in summer, winter blue. Yet when it's hot they put on sunhats, and when it's cold they hood themselves in bits of blanket. Given all this hatting and hooding, why do they shave their heads? It's absolutely senseless. Again, there are some who, using a sawlike instrument called a comb, part their hair down the middle and look as pleased as Punch with the result. Others rake out an artificial separation of the hair three-sevenths of the way across their cranial bones, and some of these extend that scraped division right over the top of their skulls so that the hair flops out at the back like false banana-leaves. Some have the hair on their crowns shorn flat but cut the hair at the sides, both left and right, to hang down straight. This creation of a square frame for a round head makes them look, if they can be said to look like anything, as though they were staring out on the world through a cedar-hedge just trimmed by a maniac gardener. In addition to these styles there are those based on cutting every hair to a standard length: the five-inch cut, the three-inch cut and even the one-inch cut. Who knows, if such close cropping is continued, they'll finish up with a cut inside their skulls. Maybe the minus-one-inch cut, even a minus-three-inch cut will be the ultimate fashion. At all events I cannot understand why mankind becomes enslaved to such fool fads.

Why, for instance, do they use two legs when they all have four available? Such waste of natural resources! If they used four legs to get about, they'd all be a great deal nippier: nevertheless they persist in the folly of using only two and leave the other pair just hanging from their shoulders like a couple of dried codfish that someone brought round as a present. One can only deduce that human beings, having so very much more spare time than do cats, lighten their natural boredom by putting their minds to thinking up such nonsenses. The odd thing is not simply that these creatures of endless leisure assure each other, whenever two of them get together, of just how busy they are, but that their faces do in fact look busy. Indeed they look so fussed that one wonders just how many men get eaten by their business. I sometimes hear them say, when they have the good fortune to make my acquaintance, how nice and easy life could be if one lived it like a cat. If they really want their lives to be nice and easy, it's already in their own good power to make them so. Nothing stands in the way. Nobody insists that they should fuss about as they do. It is entirely of their own free will that they make more engagements than they can possibly keep and then complain about being so horribly busy. Men who build themselves red-hot fires shouldn't complain of the heat. Even we cats, if we had to think up twenty different ways of scissoring our fur, would not for long remain as carefree as we are. Anyone who wants to be carefree must train himself to be, like me, able to wear a fur coat in the summer. Still . . . I must admit it is a little hot. Really, it is too hot, a fur coat in the summer.

In this appalling heat I can't even get that afternoon nap which is my sole and special pleasure. How then shall I while the time away? Since I have long neglected my study of human society, I thought I might usefully devote a few hours to watching them toiling and moiling away in their usual freakish fashions. Unfortunately, my master's character, at least in the matter of napping, is more than a little aluroid. He takes his afternoon siestas no less seriously than I do and, since the summer holidays began, he has not done a stroke of what humans would call work. Thus, however closely I may observe him, I should learn nothing new about the human condition. If only someone like Waverhouse would drop in, then there'd be some chance of a twitch in my master's depressingly dyspeptic skin, some hope of him stirring from his catlike languor. Just as I was thinking it is indeed about time that Waverhouse dropped round, I hear the sound of somebody splashing water in the bathroom. And it's not just splashing water that I hear, for the splasher punctuates his aquatics with loud expressions of his appreciation. "Perfect. How wonderfully refreshing. One more bucketful, if you please!" The voice rings brashly through the house. There's only one man in the world who would speak so loudly and who would make himself, unbidden, so very much at home in my master's dwelling. It must, thank God, be Waverhouse.

I was just thinking "Well, at least today I shall be eased of half the long day's tedium," when the man himself walks straight into the living-room. His shoulders re-covered beneath kimono sleeves, he's wiping sweat from his face as, without any ceremony at all, he pitches his hat down on the matting and calls out "Hello there. Tell me, Mrs. Sneaze, how's your husband bearing up today?" Mrs. Sneaze had been comfortably asleep in the next room. Hunkered down on her knees with her gormless face bent over onto her sewing-box, she was shocked awake as Waverhouse's yelpings pierced deep into her ears. When, trying to lever her sleepy eyes wide open, she came into the room, Waverhouse, already seated in his fine linen kimono, was happily fanning himself.

"Good afternoon," she says and, still looking somewhat confused, almost shyly adds "I'd no idea you were here." As she bowed in greeting a bead of sweat glissades to gather at the tip of her nose.

"I've only this minute arrived. With your servant's kind assistance I've just been having a most splendid shower in the bathroom. As a result I now feel greatly refreshed. Hot, though, isn't it?"

"Very hot. These last few days one's been perspiring even when sitting still. . . . But you look well as ever. . . ." Mrs. Sneaze has not yet wiped the sweat-drop from her nose.

"Thank you, yes I am. Our usual spells of heat hardly affect me at all, but this recent weather has been something special. One can't help feeling sluggish."

"How very true. I've never before felt need of a nap but in this weather, being so very hot . . ."

"You had a nap? That's good. If one could only sleep during the day-time and then still sleep at night . . . why, nothing could be more wonderful." As always, he rattles along as the mood of the moment takes him. He seems, however, this time faintly dissatisfied with what's popped out of his mouth, for he hurries to add "Take me, for example. By nature I need no sleep. Consequently, when I see a man like Sneaze who is invariably sleeping whenever I call, I feel distinctly envious. Well, I expect such heat is pretty rough on a dyspeptic. On days like this even a healthy person feels too tired to balance his head on his shoulders. However, since one's head is fixed tight, one can't just wrench it off." Rather unusually, Waverhouse seems uncertain what to do with his head. "Now you, Mrs. Sneaze, with all that hair on your head, don't you find it hard even to sit up? The weight of your chignon alone must leave you aching to lie down."

Mrs. Sneaze, thinking that Waverhouse is referring again to her nap by drawing attention to her disordered hair, giggles with embarrassment. Touching her hand to her hair, she mumbles "How unkind you are!"

Waverhouse, totally unconscious of her reaction, goes off at a tangent. "D'you know," he says, "yesterday I tried to fry an egg on the roof."

"How's that?"

"The roof-tiles were so marvelously baking-hot that I thought it a pity not to make practical use of them. So I buttered a tile and broke an egg onto it."

"Gracious me!"

"But the sun, you know, let me down. Even though I waited for ages, the egg was barely half-done. So I went downstairs to read the newspapers. Then a friend dropped in, and somehow I forgot about the egg. It was only this morning that I suddenly remembered and, thinking it must be done by now, went up to look at it."

"How was it?"

"Far from being ready to eat, it had gone completely runny. In fact, it had run away, all down the side of the house."

"Oh dear." Mrs. Sneaze frowned to show she was impressed.

"But isn't it strange that all through the hot season the weather was so cool and then it should turn so hot now."

"Yes, indeed. Right up until recently we've been shivering in our summer clothes and then, quite suddenly, the day before yesterday, this awful heat began."

"Crabs walk sideways but this year's weather walks backward. Maybe it's trying to teach us the truth of that Chinese saying that sometimes it is reasonable to act contrary to reason."

"Come again," says Mrs. Sneaze who's not much cop on Chinese proverbs.

"It was nothing. The fact is that the way this weather is retrogressing is really just like Hercules' bull." Carried away on the tide of his crankiness, Waverhouse starts making ever more odd remarks. Inevitably, my master's wife, marooned in ignorance, is left behind as Waverhouse drifts off beyond the horizons of her comprehension. However, having so recently burnt her fingers over that bit of unreasonable Chinese reason, she was not out looking for a further scorching. So "Oh," she says, and sits silent. Which doesn't, of course, suit Waverhouse. He hasn't gone to the trouble of dragging in Hercules' bull not to be asked about it.

"Mrs. Sneaze," he says, driven to the direct question, "do you know about Hercules' bull?"

"No," she says, "I don't."

"Ah, well if you don't, shall I tell you about it?"

Since she can hardly ask him to shut up, "Please do," she answers.

"One day in ancient times Hercules was leading a bull along."

"This Hercules, was he some sort of cowherd?"

"Oh no, not a cowherd. Indeed he was neither a cowherd nor yet the owner of a chain of butcher-shops. In those far days there were, in fact, no butcher-shops in Greece."

"Ah! so it's a Greek story? You should've told me so at the start. . . ." At least Mrs. Sneaze has shown that she knows that Greece is the name of a country.

"But I mentioned Hercules, didn't I?"

"Is Hercules another name for Greece?"

"Well, Hercules was a Greek hero."

"No wonder I didn't know his name! Well, what did he do?"

"Like you, dear lady, he felt sleepy. And in fact he fell asleep. . . ."

"Really! Mr. Waverhouse!"

"And while he slept, along came Vulcan's son."

"Now who's this Vulcan fellow?"

"Vulcan was a blacksmith, and his son stole Hercules' bull. But in a rather special way. Can you guess what he did? He dragged the bull off by its tail. Well, when Hercules woke up he began searching for his bull and bellowing 'Bull, where are you?' But he couldn't find it and he couldn't track it down because, you see, the beast had been hauled off backward so there weren't any hoof-marks pointing where it had gone. Pretty smart, don't you agree? For a blacksmith's son?" Dragged off track by his own tale, Waverhouse has already forgotten that he had been discussing the unseasonable heat.

"By the way," he rattled on, "what's your husband doing? Taking his usual nap? When such noddings-off are mentioned in Chinese poetry they sound refined, even romantic; but when, as in your husband's case, they happen day in, day out, the whole concept becomes vulgarized. He has reduced an eternal elegance of life to a daily form of fragmentary death. Forgive my asking you," he brings his speech to a sudden conclusion, "but please do go and wake him up."

Mrs. Sneaze seems to agree with the Waverhouse view of naps as a form of piecemeal perishing for, as she gets to her feet, she says "Indeed he's pretty far gone. Of course it's bad for his health. Especially right on top of his lunch."

"Talking of lunch, the fact is I've not had mine yet." Waverhouse drops broad hints composedly, magnanimously, as though they were pearls of wisdom.

"Oh, I am sorry. I never thought of it. It's lunch-time, of course. . . . Well, would you perhaps like some rice, pickles, seaweed, things like that, and a little hot tea?"

"No thanks. I can manage without them."

"Well, as we hadn't realized you would be honoring us today, we've nothing special we can offer you." Not unnaturally, Mrs. Sneaze responds with an edge of sarcasm.

Which is all quite wasted on Waverhouse. "No and indeed no," he imperturbably replies, "neither with hot tea nor with heated water. On my way here, I ordered a lunch to be sent to your house and that's what I'm going to eat." In his most matter-of-fact manner Waverhouse states his quite outrageous actions.

Mrs. Sneaze said "Oh!" But in that one gasped sound three separate ohs were mingled: her oh of blank surprise, her oh of piqued annoyance and her oh of gratified relief. At which moment my master comes tottering in from the study. He had just begun to doze off into sleep when it became so unusually noisy that he was hauled back into consciousness like something being scraped against its natural grain. "You're a rowdy fellow," he grumbles sourly through his yawns. "Always the same. Just when I was getting off to sleep, feeling so pleasant and relaxed . . ."

"A-ha! so you're awake! I'm extremely sorry to have disturbed your heavenly repose, but missing it just once in a while may even do you good. Please come and be seated." Waverhouse makes himself an agreeable host to my master in my master's house. My master sits down without a word: and, taking a cigarette from a box of wooden crazy-work, begins to puff at it. Then, happening to notice the hat which Waverhouse had tossed away into a corner, he observes "I see you've bought a hat."

fetches it and holds it proudly out for the
Sneazes to inspect.

"Oh, how pretty. It's very closely woven.
And so soft." Mrs. Sneaze strokes it almost
greedily.

"This hat, dear lady, is a handy hat. And as
obedient as a man could wish. Look." He
clenched his hand into a knobbly fist and
drove it sharply into the side of his precious
panama. A fist-shaped dent remained, but
before Mrs. Sneaze could finish her gasp of
surprise, Waverhouse whipped his hand inside
the hat, gave it a sharpish shove, and the hat
popped back into shape. He then grasped the
hat by opposite sides of its brim and squashed
it flat as dough beneath a rolling-pin. Next he
rolled it up, as one might roll a light straw
mat. Finally, saying "Didn't I say it was
handy," he tucked it away into the breast-fold
of his kimono.

"How extraordinary!" Mrs. Sneaze marvels
as if she were watching that master-magician
Kitensai Shoichi performing one of his most
dazzling sleights of hand. Waverhouse himself
appears to be bitten by the spirit of his own
act for, producing from his left-hand sleeve
the tube of hat he'd thrust into the breast of
his kimono, he announces "Not a scratch
upon it." He then bats the hat back into its
original shape and, sticking his forefinger into
its crown, spins it around like a conjuror's
plate. I thought the act was over, but Waverhouse proceeded neatly to flip his whirling

headgear over his head and onto the floor behind him, where, as the climax of his performance, he sat down squarely on it with a heavy solid whump.

"You're sure it's all right?" Even my master looks somewhat concerned. Mrs. Sneaze, genuinely anxious, squeaks "Please, you'd better stop. It would be terrible to spoil so fine a hat."

Only its owner wants to keep going. "But it can't be spoiled. That's the wonder of it." He heaves the crumpled object out from under his bottom and jams it on his head. It sprang back into shape.

"Indeed it's a very strong hat. Isn't it extraordinary? Quite amazing." Mrs. Sneaze is more and more impressed.

"Oh, there's nothing extraordinary about it. It's just that kind of hat," says Waverhouse smirking out from under its brim.

A moment later Mrs. Sneaze turns to her husband. "I think you too had better buy a hat like that."

"But he's already got a splendid boater."

"Just the other day the children trampled on it and it's all squashed out of shape." Mrs. Sneaze persists.

"Oh dear. That was a pity."

"That's why I think he should buy a hat like yours, strong and splendiferous." She has no idea what panama hats can cost, so nothing moderates the urgency of her proddings. "Really, my dear, you must get one, just like this. . . ."

At this point Waverhouse produces from his right sleeve a pair of scissors in a scarlet sheath. "Mrs. Sneaze," he says, "forget the hat for a moment and take a look at these scissors. They, too, are fantastically handy. You can use them in fourteen different ways." If it hadn't been for those scissors my master would have succumbed to wifely pressure in the matter of the hat. He was extremely lucky that the inborn female sense of curiosity diverted his wife's attention. It crossed my mind that Waverhouse had acted of intent, helpfully and tactfully; but after careful consideration I've concluded that it was pure good luck that saved my master from painful outlay on a panama hat.

No sooner has Mrs. Sneaze responded with a "What are the fourteen ways?" than Waverhouse is off again in triumphantly full flow. "I shall explain each of them: so listen carefully. All right? You see here a crescent-shaped opening? One sticks one's cigar in here to nip its lip-end before smoking. This gadget down here by the handle can cut through wire as though it were mere noodle. Now if you put the scissors flat down upon paper, there's a ruler for you. Here, on the back-edge of this blade, there's a scale engraved so the scissors can be used as a measure. Over here there's a file for one's fingernails. Right? Now then, if you push this blade-tip out, you can twist it round and round to drive screws. Thus, it serves as a hammer. And you can use this blade-tip to lever open with the greatest of ease even the most carefully nailed lid. Furthermore, the end of this other blade, being ground to so fine a point, makes an excellent gimlet. With this thing you can scrape out any mistakes in your writing. And finally, if you take the whole thing to pieces, you get a perfectly good knife. Now, Mrs. Sneaze, there's actually one more especially interesting feature. Here in the handle there's a tiny ball about the size of a fly. You see it? Well, take a peep right into it."

"No. I'd rather not. I'm sure you're going to make fun of me again."

"I'm grieved that you should have so little confidence in me. But, just this once, take me at my word and have a little look. No? Oh, please, just one quick squint." He handed her the scissors.

Mrs. Sneaze takes them very gingerly and, setting her eyeball close to the magic spot, does her best to see into it.

"Well?"

"Nothing. It's all black."

"All black? That won't do. Turn a little toward the paper-window and look against the light. Don't tilt the scissors like that. Right, that's it. Now you can see, can't you?"

"Oh, my! It's a photograph, isn't it? How can a tiny photograph be fixed in here?"

"That's what's so remarkable." Mrs. Sneaze and Waverhouse are now absorbed in their conversation. My master, silent now for some time but intrigued by the idea of the photograph, seems suddenly possessed by an urge to see it. He asks his wife to let him but she, her eye still glued to the scissors, just babbles on. "How very lovely. What a beautiful study of the nude." She won't be parted from the scissors.

"Come on, let me see it."

"You wait. What lovely tresses, all the way down to her hips. How movingly her face is lifted. Rather a tall girl, I'd say, but indeed a beauty!"

"Damn it, let me see." My master, now distinctly narked, flares up at his wife.

"There you are then. Gawp away to your heart's content." As she was handing the scissors over, the servant trundles in from the kitchen with an announcement that Waverhouse's meal has been delivered. Indeed she carries with her two lidded bamboo-plates loaded with cold buckwheat noodles.

"Aha," says Waverhouse, "so here, Mrs. Sneaze, is the lunch I bought myself. With your permission, I propose to eat it now." He bows respectfully. As he seems to have spoken half in earnest and half in jest, Mrs. Sneaze is at a loss how best to answer, so she just says lightly "Please do," and settles back to watch.

At long last my master drags his eyes away from the photograph and remarks "In weather as hot as this, noodles are bad for one's health."

"No danger. What one likes seldom upsets one. In fact I've heard," says Waverhouse, lifting one of the lids, "that a little of what you fancy does you good." He appears satisfied by what he's seen on the plate for he goes straight on to observe "In my opinion noodles that have been left to stand are, like heavily bearded men, never to be relied upon." He adds green horse-radish to his dish of soy-sauce and stirs away like mad.

"Steady on," says my master in genuinely anxious tones, "if you put in that much spice it'll be too hot to eat."

"Noodles must be eaten with soy-sauce and green horse-radish. I bet you don't even like noodles."

"I do indeed. The normal kind."

"That's the stuff for pack-horse drivers. A man insensitive to cold buckwheat noodles spiced like this is a man devoutly to be pitied." So saying, Waverhouse digs his cedar-wood chopsticks deep into the mass of noodles, scoops up a hefty helping and lifts it some two inches. "Did you know, Mrs. Sneaze, that there are several styles for eating noodles? Raw beginners always use too much sauce and then they munch this delicacy like so many cattle chewing the cud. That way, the exquisite savor of the noodles is inevitably lost. The correct procedure is to scoop them up like this. . . ." Waverhouse raises his chopsticks above the bamboo plate until a foot-long curtain of noodles dangles in the air. He looks down at the plate to check that he's lifted his lading clear of the plate but finds a

dozen or so of the tail-ends still lying coiled
within it.

"What very long noodles! Look, Mrs.
Sneaze, aren't they the longest that you ever
saw?" Waverhouse demands that his audience
should participate, if only by interjections.

"Indeed, they are lengthy!" she answers, as
if impressed by his dissertation.

"Now, you dip just one-third of these long
strands in the sauce, then swallow them in a
single gulp. You mustn't chew them. Masti-
cation destroys their unique flavor. The
whole point of noodles is in the way they
slither down one's throat." He thereupon
raises his chopsticks to a dramatic height and
the ends of the longest strands at last swing
clear of the plate. Then, as he starts to lower
his arm again, the tail-ends of the noodles
slowly start submerging into the sauce-dish
held in his left hand. Which, in accordance
with Archimedes' Law, causes the sauce
slowly to rise in the dish as its volume is dis-
placed by noodles. However, since the dish
was originally eight-tenths full of sauce, the
level of the liquid reached its brim before
Waverhouse could get even one-quarter, let
alone the connoisseur's one-third, of the
length of his wriggling noodles into the
sauce. The chopsticks appear paralyzed about
five inches above the dish and so remain for
an awkward pause while Waverhouse considers his dilemma. If he lowers the noodles
one more fraction of an inch, the sauce must

overflow; but if he does not lower them, he must fail to conform with the standards he has established for the proper style of stuffing oneself with noodles. No wonder he looks moithered and half-hesitates. Then, suddenly, jerking his head and neck forward and downward like a striking snake, he jabbed his mouth at the chopsticks. There was a slushy slurping sound, his throttle surged and receded once or twice and the noodles were all gone. A few tears oozed from the corners of his eyes. To this day I am not sure whether those tear-drops were a tribute to the strength of the green horse-radish or evidence of the painful effort such gurgitation must involve.

"What an extraordinary performance! How on earth," enquires my flabbergasted master, "do you contrive to gulp down such a mass of vermicelli in one consuming go?"

"Amazing, isn't he!" Mrs. Sneaze is equally lost in admiration.

Waverhouse says nothing, puts down the chopsticks and pats his chest an easing couple of times. "Well, Mrs. Sneaze," he eventually answers, "a plate of noodles should be consumed in three and a half, at most in four, mouthfuls. If you drag out the process longer than that, the noodles will not taste their best." He wipes his face with a handkerchief and sits back to take a well-earned breather.

At this point who should walk in but Coldmoon. His feet are soiled with summer dust but, for no reason I can offer, despite the broiling heat he's wearing a winter hat.

"Hallo! Here comes our handsome hero! However, since I'm still in the middle of eating, you must excuse me." Waverhouse, totally unabashed, settles down to finishing off the noodles. This time, rather sensibly, he makes no effort to give a repeat performance as a vermicelli virtuoso, and is consequently spared the indignities of needing support from handkerchiefs and breathers between mouthfuls. Eating normally he empties both the bamboo plates in a matter of minutes.

"Coldmoon," says my master, "how's your thesis coming along?" And Waverhouse adds "Since the delectable Miss Goldfield is yearning to be yours, you should in common kindness submit the finished text as fast as possible."

Coldmoon breaks as usual into his disconcertingly idiot grin. "Inasmuch as waiting is a cruelty to her, I'd like indeed to finish it quickly," he replies, "but the nature of its subject is such that a great deal of drudging research is unavoidable." He spoke with measured seriousness of things he couldn't possibly himself be taking seriously.

"Quite so," says Waverhouse adopting Coldmoon's style with contrapuntal skill. "The subject being what it is, naturally it cannot be handled just as Coldmoon wishes. Nevertheless, that nasality her mother being the snorter that she is, naturally it would be prudent to trim one's sails to the way she blows."

The only relatively sensible comment

comes from my master. "What did you say was the subject of your thesis?"

"It is entitled 'The Effects of Ultraviolet Rays upon Galvanic Action in the Eyeball of the Frog.'"

"Remarkable. Just what one might expect from Coldmoon. I like both the rhythm and the substantial originality of that last bit, the electrifying shock in that 'eyeball of the frog.' How about it, Sneaze? Ought we not to inform the Goldfields of at least the title before our scholar finishes his paper?"

My master, disregarding these waggeries from Waverhouse, asks Coldmoon "Can such a subject really involve much drudgery of research?"

"Oh yes, it's a complicated question. For one thing, the structure of the lens in the eyeball of the frog is by no means simple. Hundreds, even thousands, of experiments will have to be carried out. For a start I'm planning to construct a round glass ball."

"A glass ball? Surely, you could find one quite easily in a glass-shop?"

"Oh, no; far from it," says Coldmoon, throwing out his chest a little. "To begin with, things like circles and straight lines are pure geometrical concepts, and neither actual circles nor actual straight lines can, in this imperfect world, ever realize such idealities."

"If they can never exist, hadn't you better abandon the attempt to create them?" butts in Waverhouse.

"Well, I thought I'd begin by making a

ball suitable for my experiments and, in fact, I started on it the other day."

"And have you finished it?" asks my master as if the task were an easy matter.

"How could I?" says Coldmoon: but then, realizing perhaps that he's getting close to self-contradiction, hurries on to explain. "It's really frightfully difficult. After I've filed it for some time, I notice that the radius on one side is too long, so I grind it fractionally shorter: but this leads on to trouble; because now I find the radius on the other side excessive. When, with great effort I grind that excess off, the entire ball becomes misshapen. After I've at last corrected that distortion, I discover that the diametrical dimensions have, somehow or other, once more gone agley. The glass ball, originally the size of an apple, soon becomes a strawberry and, as I patiently struggle for perfection, it rapidly shrinks to no more than a bean. Even then, it's not a perfect sphere. Believe me, I have striven. . . . I have dedicated my whole life to the grinding of glass balls. Since New Year's Day no less than six of them, admittedly of differing sizes, have melted away to nothing in these hands. . . ." He speaks with such rare passion that no one could say whether or not he's telling the truth.

"Where do you do this grinding?"

"In the university laboratory of course. I start grinding in the morning. I take a short rest for lunch, and then continue grinding till the light fails. It's not an easy job."

"D'you mean to say that you go down to the university day after day, including Sundays, simply to grind glass balls? Is that what keeps you, as you're always telling us, so inexorably busy?"

"That's correct. At this stage in my studies I have no choice but to grind glass balls morning, noon and night."

"I seem to recall," says Waverhouse, now very much in his element, "a Kabuki play in which one character gains his ends by disguising himself as a gardener." He strikes an attitude and quotes " 'As I was luckily brought up among civilian non-officials, no one knows my face: so I enter as a cultivator of chrysanthemums.' You, Coldmoon, seem bent on gaining your ends disguised as a cultivator of crystals. For I'm sure that when the mother of all noses learns of your ardor, your single-minded dedication to your work, your selfless devotion to the grinding of glass balls, she cannot fail to warm toward you. Incidentally, the other day I had some work to do in the university library and, as I was leaving, I chanced to bump into an old colleague, Knarle-Damson, at the door. Thinking it peculiar that, years after his graduation, he should still be using the library, I said to him 'Knarle-Damson,' I said, 'I'm most impressed, Knarle-Damson, to find you still imbibing at the fount of learning.' He gave me a very odd look and explained that, far from wanting to consult a book, he'd been caught short as he passed the university and

had just popped in for a pee. A curious use
for a seat of learning. However, it's just
occurred to me that you and Knarle-Damson
both exemplify, though in contrasting styles,
how to misuse a university. You will, of
course, have read that Chinese classic which
is constructed from pairs of parallel anec-
dotes, one ancient and one modern, about
famous men. I am proposing to bring out a
New Selection along similar lines and, with
your permission, will include therein a short
section on glass balls and urinals."

My master, however, took a more serious
view of the matter. "It's all very well," he
said, "to pass your days frotting away at
glass but when do you expect to finish your
thesis and get your doctorate?"

"At my present rate of progress, maybe in
ten years." Coldmoon seems far less concerned than my master about the doctorate.

"Ten years, eh? I think you'd better bring
your grinding to a halt rather sooner than
that."

"Ten years is an optimistic estimate. It
could well take me twenty."

"That's terrible. You can't, then, hope for
a doctorate for a long time."

"No. Of course I'd be only too happy to
get it quickly and so set the young lady's mind
at rest; but until I've got the glass ball properly ground, I can't even launch out on my
first experiment." Coldmoon's voice trailed
off into silence as though his mind were staring into the lens of a frog's eyeball but, after

a brief pause, he continued. "There's no need, you know, to get so worried about it. The Goldfields are fully aware that I do nothing but grind away at these glass balls. As a matter of fact, I gave them a fairly detailed explanation when I saw them just a few days back." He smiled in quiet complacence.

Mrs. Sneaze who, though hardly understanding a word of it, has been listening to the three men's conversation, interjects in a puzzled voice "But the whole Goldfield family has been away at the seaside, out at Oiso, since last month."

This flummoxes even Coldmoon, but he maintains a pretense of innocence. "How very odd," he says, "I can't understand it."

There are occasions when Waverhouse fulfils a useful social function. When a conversation flags, when one is embarrassed, when one becomes sleepy, when one is troubled, then, as on all other occasions, Waverhouse can be relied upon to have something immediate and diverting to say. "To have met someone a few days back in Tokyo who had gone to Oiso last month is engagingly mysterious. It is an example, is it not, of the exchange of souls. Such a phenomenon is likely to occur when the sentiment of requited love is particularly poignant. When one hears of such a happening, it sounds like a dream; but, even if it is a dream, it is a dream more actual than reality. For someone like you, Mrs. Sneaze, who were married to Sneaze not because you loved him or because he loved

you to understand the extraordinary nature of
love: so it is only natural that you should find
odd the disparities you mentioned. . . ."

"I don't know why you should say such
nasty things. Why are you always getting at
me like this?" Mrs. Sneaze rounds snappishly
on Waverhouse.

"What's more, you yourself don't look like
a man who has any experience of the pangs
of love." My master brings up reinforcements
in surprising support of the front-line position manned by his wife.

"Well, since all my love-affairs were over
long before the nine days back that might
have made them wonders, you doubtless
don't remember them. But it remains a fact
that it was a disappointment in love that has
made me, to this day, a lonely bachelor."
Waverhouse leveled a steady look upon each
of his listeners, one after the other.

It was Mrs. Sneaze who laughed, though
she added "But how interesting."

My master said "Bosh," and turned to
stare off into the garden.

Coldmoon, though he grinned, said po-
litely "I would like, for my own future benefit, to hear the story of your ancient love."

"My story, too, contains elements of the
mysterious. So much so that, if he were not
lamentably dead, it must have moved the
interest of the late Lafcadio Hearn. I am, I
must confess, a little reluctant to tell this
painful tale but, since you insist, I'll confide

in you all on the sole condition that you listen carefully to the very end." They promised, and he starts.

"As well as I can recollect . . . it was . . . hum . . . how many years ago was it, I wonder. . . . Never mind, let's say it was maybe fifteen or sixteen years ago."

"Incorrigible," snorts my master.

"You do have a very poor memory, don't you, Mr. Waverhouse?" Mrs. Sneaze puts in a jabbing oar.

Coldmoon is the only person who, keeping the promise, says nothing but wears the expression of a man eagerly waiting for the remainder of a story.

"Anyway it was in the winter, some years back. Having passed through the Valley of the Bamboo Shoots at Kambara in Echigo, I was climbing up through the Pass of the Octopus Trap on my way to the Aizu territory."

"What odd-named places!" My master interrupts again.

"Oh, do keep quiet and listen. This is getting interesting." Mrs. Sneaze reins back her husband.

"Unfortunately it was getting dark. I lost my way. I was hungry. So, in the end, I was obliged to knock at the door of a hut way up in the middle of the Pass. Explaining my predicament, I begged for a night's lodging. And do you know, the minute that I saw the face of the girl who, thrusting a lit candle out toward me, answered 'Of course, please enter,' my whole body began to tremble. Since that moment I've been very acutely conscious of the supernatural power of that blind force we call love."

"Fancy that," says Mrs. Sneaze. "Are there really, I wonder, many beautiful girls living up there in those god-forsaken mountains?"

"It hardly matters that I found her in the mountains. It might just as well have been beside the seaside. But, oh Mrs. Sneaze, would that you could have seen her, if only for a glance. . . . She wore her hair in the high-dressed fashion of a marriageable girl. . . ."

Mrs. Sneaze, rendered speechless by the wonder of it all, gives vent to a long-drawn sigh.

"On entering the hut, I found a big fireplace sunk in the center of an eight-mat room; and soon the four of us—the girl, her grandfather, her grandmother and myself—were sitting comfortably around it. They said I must be very hungry. And I was. Very. So I asked for some food, anything, no matter what, so long as I might have it quickly. The old man said 'It's seldom we have visitors, so let's prepare snake-rice in honor of our guest.' Now then, this is where I come to the story of my disappointment in love; so listen carefully."

"Of course we'll listen carefully," says

Coldmoon, "but I find it hard to believe that even out in the wilds of Echigo there are snakes around in the winter."

"Well, that's a fair observation. But in a romantic story such as this, one shouldn't be too scrupulous over the logic of its details. Why, in one of Kyoka's novels, you'll find a crab crawling out of the snow."

"I see," said Coldmoon who thereupon resumed his serious attitude of listening.

"In those days I was outstandingly capable, really in the champion class, of eating ugly foods: but, being more or less wearied of locusts, slugs, red frogs and such like, I thought snake-rice sounded like a welcome change. So I told the old man I'd be delighted. He then set a pot on the fire and put some rice inside it. Slowly it began to cook. The only oddity was that there were about ten holes of various sizes in the lid of the pot. Through these holes, the steam came fuffing up. I was really fascinated by the effect and I remember thinking how ingenious these country people were. Just then, the old man suddenly stood up and went out of the hut. A while later, he came back with a large basket under his arm and, when he put it casually down beside the hearth, I took a look inside. Well, there they were. Snakes, and all of them long ones, coiled up tight, as Coldmoon will appreciate, in their winter torpor."

"Please stop talking about such nasty things. It's quite revolting," says Mrs. Sneaze with a girlish shudder.

"Oh I can't possibly stop, for all these matters lie at the bottom of my broken-heartedness. Well, by and by, the old man lifted the pot's lid with his left hand while with his other he nimbly grabbed up a wad of snakes from the basket. He threw them into the pot and popped the lid back on. And I must admit that, though I'm neither squeamish nor particularly scared of snakes, the old man's nonchalant action did, at that moment, leave me gasping."

"Oh, please do stop. I can't stand gruesome stories." Mrs. Sneaze is actually quite frightened.

"Very soon now I'll be coming to the broken-hearted bit, so please just do be patient. Well, barely a minute had passed when, to my great surprise, a snake's head popped out of a hole in the lid. I'd barely realized what it was before another one popped its face out from a neighboring hole; and I'd barely registered that second head before another and another and another erupted into view until the whole lid was studded with snakes' faces."

"Why did they stick their heads out?" asks my master.

"Because, in agony, they were trying to crawl away from the heat building up inside the pot. After a while the old man said, speaking, naturally, in his local dialect, something like 'Right then, give 'em the old heave-ho.' His wife said 'Aye' and the girl said 'Yes' and each of them, grasping a snake's head firmly, gave it a savage yank. While the flesh remained in the pot, the head and a length of bones came waggling free in their hands."

"What you might call boned snake?" asks Coldmoon with a laugh.

"Yes, indeed. Boned, or even spineless. But wasn't it all exceedingly clever? They lifted the lid, took a ladle, stirred the rice and the snake-flesh into one great wonderful mish-mash and then invited me to tuck in."

"Did you actually eat it?" asks my master in a slightly edgy sort of voice.

His wife makes a sour face and grumblingly complains. "I do so wish you'd all stop talking about it. I'm feeling sick right down to my stomach, and I shan't dare eat for days."

"You only say that, Mrs. Sneaze, because you've never had the luck to taste snake-rice. If you but tried it once, you'd never forget its exquisite flavor."

"Never. Nothing on earth could induce me to touch the nasty stuff."

"Anyway, I dined well. I forgot the bitter cold. I studied the girl's face to my heart's content and, though I could happily have stared at her forever, when they suggested I should go to sleep, I remembered that I was in fact dog-tired from my traveling. So I took their advice and lay down; and before long everything blurred and I was fast asleep."

"And what happened then?" This time it's Mrs. Sneaze who urges him to continue.

"When I woke up next morning, heart-ache had set in."

"No, nothing special happened to me. I just woke up and, while I was smoking a cigarette, I chanced to look out through the back-window: and there I saw, washing its face in the water flowing from a bamboo-pipe, someone bald as a kettle."

"The old man," asks my master, "or the old woman?"

"At first I couldn't tell. I sat there watching it in vague distaste for quite some time and, when at last the kettle turned towards me, I got the shock of my life. For it was the girl to whom I had already lost my heart."

"But you said earlier that she wore her hair in the style of a marriageable girl," my master promptly objects.

"The night before, unmitigated beauty: in the morning, unmitigated kettle."

"Really! What balderdash will you trot out next." As is usual when he feels put out, my master stares at the ceiling.

"Naturally I was most deeply shocked, even a little frightened: but, making myself inconspicuous, I continued to watch. At long last the kettle finished washing its face, featly donned the wig waiting on a near-by stone and then came tripping primly back to the hut. I understood everything. But though I understood, I have from that moment been a man incurably wretched, a man with a broken heart."

"The silliest broken heart that ever was.

Observe, my dear Coldmoon, how gay and lively he contrives to be despite his broken heart." Turning toward Coldmoon, my master registers his low opinion of his friend's disastrous love-affair.

"But," says Coldmoon, "if the girl had not been bald and if Waverhouse had brought her back with him to Tokyo, he might be now yet livelier than he is. The fact remains that it is infinitely pitiable that the young lady happened to be bald. But tell me, Waverhouse, how did it come about that a girl so young should have lost her hair?"

"Well, naturally I've thought about that too; and I'm certain now that the depilation must be due entirely to over-indulgence in snake-rice. It goes to the head, you know. It drives the blood upward, damaging the capillaries in the follicles of the scalp."

"I'm so glad nothing so terrible happened to you," says Mrs. Sneaze with an undertone of sarcasm.

"It is true that I was spared the affliction of going bald: but instead, as you can see, I have become a presbyope." Taking off his gold-rimmed spectacles, he polishes them carefully with his pocket handkerchief.

There was a short silence. To be a presbyope sounded so awful that none dared ask for an explanation. But my master, possibly being made of sterner stuff, possibly because he knows that near-sightedness is more often caused by the passing of the years than by one night's meal of snake-rice, was not yet done.

"I seem to remember," he eventually said, "that you mentioned some mystery that would have moved the interest of Lafcadio Hearn. What mystery?"

"Did she buy the wig or simply pick it up; and, if she picked it up, where? That," said Waverhouse, replacing his spectacles on his nose, "is the mystery. To this day I cannot work it out."

"It's just like listening to a comic story-teller," says Mrs. Sneaze.

As Waverhouse's improbable tale had come to its conclusion, I thought he might shut up. But no. He appears by nature incapable of keeping quiet unless actually gagged. For he's at it again already.

"My disappointment in love was, of course, a bitter experience: but had I married that heavenly girl in ignorance of kettledom, the matter would have remained a lifelong cause of friction. One has to be careful. In matters like marriage, one tends only to discover at the very last moment hidden defects in unexpected places. I therefore advise you, Coldmoon, not to waste your youth in futile yearnings or in pointless despair but to keep on grinding away at your balls of glass with an easy mind and heart."

"I'd be happy," answers Coldmoon, "to do nothing more. However, the Goldfield ladies, to my considerable botheration, do keep on at me." He grimaces in exaggerated annoyance.

"True. You are, in your case, somewhat

put upon. But there are many comic cases of people thrusting themselves forward to invite disquiet. Take, for example, the case of Knarle-Damson, that well-known piddler upon seats of learning. His was extremely odd."

"What did he do?" asks my master, entering into the swing of the conversation.

"Well, it was like this. Once upon a long, long time ago, he stayed at the East-West Inn in Shizuoka. Just for one night, mind you, but that same evening he offered marriage to one of the servants working there. I myself am pretty easy-going, but I would not find it easy to go as far as that. The fact was that in those days one of the maids at that Inn, they called her Summer, was a raving beauty; and it just so happened that she looked after Knarle-Damson's room, so he could not help but meet her."

"The meeting was no doubt fated, just like yours in that something-or-other Pass," observes my master.

"Yes, there is some resemblance between the cases. Indeed, there are obvious similarities between Knarle-Damson and myself. Anyway, he proposed to this Summer girl but, before she gave her answer, he felt a need for water-melon."

"Huh?" My master looks puzzled. And not only he; for both his wife and Coldmoon cock their heads sideways as they try to see the connection. Waverhouse disregards them all and proceeds blithely with his story.

"He summoned the girl and asked her if one could get a water-melon in Shizuoka. She replied that, though the town was not as up-to-date as Tokyo, even in Shizuoka water-melons could be had; and almost immediately she brought him a tray heaped high with slices of the fruit. So, while waiting for her answer, Knarle-Damson scoffed the lot. But before she gave her answer, Knarle-Damson got the the gripes. He groaned away like mad but, since that didn't help, he summoned the girl again and this time asked if there was a doctor available. The girl replied that, though the town was not as up-to-date as Tokyo, still, even in Shizuoka, doctors were available, and in a matter of minutes she ushered one into his room. The doctor, incidentally, had a very odd name, something like Heaven-and-Earth, anyway something obviously cribbed for effect from the Chinese classics. Well, next morning when Knarle-Damson woke up, he was delighted to find his gut-ache gone; and, some fifteen minutes before he was due to leave, he again summoned the Summer girl and asked for her answer to his proposal of marriage. The girl replied with laughter. She then said that down in Shizuoka it is possible to find doctors and water-melons at very short notice but that, even in Shizuoka, few find brides in a single night. She turned, went out of the room and that was the last he saw of her. And ever since that day, Knarle-Damson has remained, like me, a man scarred by a disappointment in love. Almost a recluse, he'll only go to a library when pressed there by his bladder. Which all goes to show the wickedness and cruelty of women."

My master, most unusually, comes out this time in strong support of Waverhouse's theme. "How right you are," he says, "how very right. Just the other day I was reading one of de Musset's plays in which some character quoted Ovid to the effect that lighter than a feather is dust; than dust, wind; than wind, woman; but than woman, nothing. A very penetrating observation, isn't it? Women are indeed the dreaded end." My master adopts an exceedingly cavalier attitude, but his wife, of course, is not going to let these flourishes pass unchallenged.

"You complain about women being light, but I can't see any particular merit in the fact that men are heavy."

"What do you mean by heavy?"

"Heavy is just heavy. Like you."

"Why d'you say I'm heavy?"

"Because you are heavy. Very heavy."

They're off on one of their crazy arguments again. For a time Waverhouse just sits there, listening with amusement to their increasingly bitter bickering but eventually he opens his mouth.

"The way you two go on at each other, hammering away till you're red in the face, is perhaps the clearest possible demonstration that you truly are husband and wife. I'm inclined to think that marriage in the old days

was a less meaningful thing than it is today."
None of his listeners could tell whether he
was teasing or complimenting his host and
hostess but, since their bickering was halted,
he could with profit just have stopped there.
But that's not the way of a Waverhouse, who
always has more to say.

"I hear that in the old days no woman
would have dreamt of answering back to her
husband. From the man's point of view it
must have been like marriage to a deaf-mute.
I wouldn't have liked that. Not one little bit.
I certainly prefer women who, like you, Mrs.
Sneaze, have the spirit to retort 'Because you
are heavy' or something else in the same vein.
If one is to be married, it would be insup-
portably boring never to have the liveliness
of an occasional spat. My mother, for instance, spent her whole life saying 'Yes' and
'You're right' to my frequently foolish
father. She lived with him for twenty or so
assenting years, and in all that stretch she
never set foot outside the house except to go
to a temple. Really, it's too pitiful. There
were, of course, advantages. Thus my mother
has the enormous satisfaction of knowing
that she knows by heart the full posthumous
names of all my family's ancestors. This
hideous sort of relationship did not exist
simply between man and wife but extended
to cover the whole range of relations between
the sexes. When I was a lad it was quite out of
the question for a young man and a young
woman even to play music together. There

was no such thing as a lovers' meeting. They couldn't even meet in the world of the spirit, like Coldmoon here, by a long-range swap of souls."

"It must have been awful," says Coldmoon with a sort of shrinking bow.

"Indeed it was. One weeps for one's ancestors. Still, women in those days were not necessarily any better behaved than the women of today. You know, Mrs. Sneaze, people talk down their noses about the depraved conduct of modern girl-students, but the truth is that things were very much worse in those so-called good old days."

"Really?" Mrs. Sneaze is serious.

"Of course. I'm not just making it up. I can prove what I say. You, Sneaze, will probably remember that when we were maybe five or six there were men going about in the streets with two panniers hanging down from each end of their shoulder-poles; and in the panniers, like so many pumpkins, they had little girls for sale. You remember?"

"I don't remember anything of the sort."

"I don't know how things were in your part of the country, but that's most certainly the way it was in Shizuoka."

"Surely not," murmurs Mrs. Sneaze.

"Do you mean that for a fact?" asks Coldmoon in a tone of voice that shows he can't quite credit it.

"For an absolute rock-hard fact. I can even remember how once my father haggled over the price of one. I must then have been about six. As my father and I were coming out of a side-street into the main thoroughfare we saw a man approaching us who was bawling out 'Girls for sale! Girls for sale! Anyone want a baby girl?' When we reached the corner of the second block in the street, we came face to face with this hawker, just in front of the draper's. Isegen's it was. Isegen is quite the biggest draper in Shizuoka with a sixty-foot frontage and five warehouses. Have a look at it the next time you're down there. It's just the same today as it was then. Quite unaltered. A fine building. The chief clerk's name is Jimbei, and he sits at his counter with the invariable expression of a man who's lost his mother only three days back. Sitting right beside Jimbei you'll find a young man of twenty-four, maybe twenty-five, whose name is Hatsu. Hatsu's very pale. He looks like one of those novices who, in demonstration of their devotion to the thirty-third priest-prince of the Shingon Sect, take nothing but buckwheat-water for twenty-one days at a stretch. And next to Hatsu there's Chodon. Chodon's the one who's hunched dejectedly above his abacus as though but yesterday he lost his home in a fire. And next to Chodon . . ."

"Come off it, Waverhouse," snaps my master. "Is this a chanting of the genealogy of your draper or is it a tale about the maiden-mongers of Shizuoka?"

"Ah yes. I was telling you the story of the maiden-mongers. As a matter of fact, there's an extremely strange story I was going to tell you about that draper's but I'll cut it out and concentrate on the sellers of little girls."

"Why not cut that too?" suggests my master.

"Oh no! I wouldn't feel right if I abandoned that story. For it provides exceedingly valuable data by which to compare the characters of modern women with those of their predecessors in the early Meiji Era. Now, as I was saying, when my father and I arrived in front of Isegen, the maiden-monger addressed my father in these terms: ' 'ow about one of these 'ere little left-overs? Take a toddler, sir, and I'll make 'er special cheap.' He's put his shoulder-pole down on the ground and is wiping sweat from his brow. In each of the two dumped panniers there's a little girl about two years old. My father says 'If they're really cheap, I might: but is this all you've got?' The man replies respectfully 'Yes, sir, I'm afraid so. Today I've sold 'em all, 'cept for these two little 'uns. Take your choice.' He holds the little girls up in his hands like, as I told you, pumpkins and he pushes them under my father's nose. My father taps on their heads as one might rap a melon and says 'Yes, they sound quite good.' The negotiations then begin in earnest and, after a great deal of chaffering, my father finally says 'That's all very well, but can you guarantee their quality?' 'Yes,' says the man. 'That 'un in the leading basket I can take me oath is sound, 'cos I've 'ad 'er all day long right in front of me own two peepers; but t'other in the back-side basket could be a wee mite cracked. I've not got eyes in the back of me 'ead, so I won't go making no promises. Tell you what, just for you, I'll knock a bit more off for that 'un.' To this day I can clearly remember every word of their dickering and, though only a nipper myself, I did then learn how insidiously cracked a little girl can be. However, in this thirty-eighth year of the Emperor's reign there's none so foolish now as to go trotting through the streets with little girls for sale; so one no longer hears people saying how those at the back, those that one can't keep one's own sharp watchful eye on, are liable to be damaged. It is consequently my opinion that, thanks to the beneficent influx of Western civilization, the conduct of women has in fact improved. What do you think, Coldmoon?"

Coldmoon hesitated, cleared his throat and then gave his opinion in a low and measured tone. "Women today, on their way to and from schools, at concerts, at charity-parties and at garden-parties, are, in effect, already selling themselves. Their light behavior is tantamount to such statements as 'Hey, how about buying me?' or 'Oh, so you're not much interested!' There is accordingly no contemporary need for hawkers or other middlemen selling on commission, and the street-cries of our modern cities are of course the poorer by the disappearance of maidenmongers shouting their wares. Such changes are bound to follow from the introduction and dissemination of modern ideas of the individual's independence. The older generation get unnecessarily worked up and moan and groan as though the world were coming to its end; but that's the trend of modern civilization and I, for one, welcome and encourage these changes. For instance, there's no need nowadays for anyone to go tapping poor tots on the skull to see if they're good enough to buy. In any case, no one ever gets anywhere in this hard world by being unduly choosey. That way, one can easily end up husbandless and, even after fifty or sixty years' assiduous search, still not be a bride."

Coldmoon, very much a bright young man of this twentieth century, spoke for his generation and, having so spoken, blew cigarette smoke into Waverhouse's face. But Waverhouse is not a man to flinch from a mere residue of burnt tobacco. "As you say," he responded, "among school-girls and young ladies nowadays their very flesh and bones are permeated with, if not actually manufactured out of, self-esteem and self-confidence; and it is indeed admirable that they should prove themselves a match for men in every possible field. Take, for instance, the girls at the high school near my house. They're terrific. Togged out in trousers, they hang themselves upside-down from iron wall-bars. Truly, it's wonderful. Every time that I look down from my upstairs window and see them catapulting about at their gymnastics, I am reminded of ancient Grecian ladies pursuing strength and beauty through the patterns of calisthenics."

"Oh no. Not the Greeks again," says my master with something like a sneer.

"It's unavoidable. It just so happens that almost everything aesthetically beautiful seems to have originated in Greece. Aesthetics and the Greeks: you speak of one and you are speaking of the other. When I see those dark-skinned girls putting their whole hearts into their gymnastics, into my mind, invariably, leaps the story of Agnodice." He's wearing his font-of-all-wisdom face as he babbles on and on.

"So you've managed to find another of those awkward names," says Coldmoon with his usual witless grin.

"Agnodice was a wonderful woman. When I look back at her across the gulf of centuries, still I am impressed. In those far days the Laws of Athens forbade women to be mid-wives. It was most inconvenient. One can easily see why Agnodice thought it unreasonable."

"What's that? What's that word?"

"Agnodice. A woman. It's a woman's name. Now this woman said to herself 'It's really lamentable that women cannot be midwives, inconvenient too. I wish to God I could become a midwife. Isn't there any way I can?' So she thought and thought, doing nothing else for three straight days and nights, and just at dawn on the third day, as

she heard the yowling of a babe new born
next door, the solution flashed upon her. She
immediately cut off her long hair, dressed
herself as a man and took to attending the
lectures on childbirth then being given by the
eminent Hierophilus. She learnt all that he
could teach and, feeling her time had come,
set up as a midwife. D'you know, Mrs.
Sneaze, she was a great success. Here, there
and everywhere yowling babies put in their
appearance; and, since they were all assisted
by Agnodice, she made a fortune. However,
the ways of Heaven are proverbially inscru-
table. For seven ups there are eight downs.
And it never rains but it pours. Her secret
was discovered. She was hauled before the
courts. And she stood in danger of the direst
punishment for breaking the Laws of
Athens."

"You sound just like a professional story-
teller," says Mrs. Sneaze.

"Aren't I good? Well then, at that point all
the women of Athens got together and signed
such an enormous round robin in support of
Agnodice that the magistrates felt unable to
ignore it. In the end she was let off, and the
Laws were changed to allow women to become midwives, and they all lived happily
ever after."

"You do know about so many things. It's
wonderful," sighs Mrs. Sneaze.

"True. I know almost everything about
almost everything. Perhaps the only thing I
don't know all about is the real extent of my

own foolishness. But even on that, I can make
a pretty good guess."

"You do say such funny things. . . ." Mrs.
Sneaze was still chortling away when the
front door-bell, its tone unchanged since the
day it was first installed, began to tinkle.

"What! another visitor!" squeaked Mrs.
Sneaze and scuttled off into the living-room.

And who should it be but our old friend
Beauchamp Blowlamp. With his arrival the
entire cast of the eccentrics who haunt my
master's house was gathered upon stage. Lest
that should sound ungracious, perhaps I
could better emphasize that sufficient eccentrics are gathered to keep a cat amused; and
it would indeed be ungracious if I were not
satisfied with that. Had I had the misfortune
to dwell in some other household, I might
have lived nine lives and never known that
such remarkable scholars, that even one such
remarkable scholar, could be found among
mankind. I count myself fortunate to be sitting here, his adopted cat-child, beside my
noble master. It is, moreover, a rare privilege
to be numbered among the disciples of Professor Sneaze: for only thus am I enabled,
comfortably lying down, to observe the manners and actions not only of my master but of
such heroic figures, such matchless warriors,
as Waverhouse, Coldmoon and the bold Sir
Beauchamp. Even in this vast city, such per-
sonages are rare; and I take it as the highest
accolade that I am accepted by them as one
of their company. It is only the consciousness

of that honor which enables me to forget the hardship of being condemned to endure this heat in a fur bag. And I am especially grateful thus to be kept amused for a whole half-day. Whenever the four of them get together like this, something entertaining is bound to transpire so I watch them respectfully from that draft-cooled place by the door to which I have retired.

"I'm afraid I haven't been round to see you for quite some time," says Beauchamp with a modest bow. His head, I notice, shines as brightly as it did the other day. Judged by his head alone, he might be taken for a second-rate actor, but the ceremonious manner in which he wears his very stiff white cotton *hakama* makes him look like nothing so much as a student-swordsman from the fencing-school of Sakakibara Kenkichi. Indeed, the only part of Beauchamp's body which looks in the least bit normal is the section between his hips and his shoulders.

"Well, how nice of you to call. In this hot weather too. Come right in." Waverhouse, as usual, plays the host in someone else's home.

"I haven't seen you for a long time, sir," Beauchamp says to him.

"Quite so. Not, I believe, since that Reading Party last spring. Are you still active in that line? Have you again performed the part of a high-class prostitute? You did it very well. I applauded you like mad. Did you notice?"

"Yes, I was much encouraged. Your kind appreciation gave me the strength to carry on till the end."

"When are you having your next meeting?" interjects my master.

"We rest during July and August but we hope to be livening up again in September. Can you suggest anything interesting we might tackle?"

"Well . . ." My master answers half-heartedly.

"Look here, Beauchamp," says Coldmoon suddenly, "Why don't you try my piece?"

"If it's yours, it must be interesting: but what's this piece you've written?"

"A drama," says Coldmoon with all the brass-faced equanimity he could muster. His three companions are dumbfounded, and stare upon him with looks of unanimous wonder.

"A drama! Good for you! A comedy or tragedy?" Beauchamp was the first to recover and find his tongue. With the utmost composure Coldmoon gives his reply.

"It's neither a comedy nor a tragedy. Since people these days are always fussing about whether a play should be old-style drama or new-style drama, I decided to invent a totally new type and have accordingly written what I call a *haiku*-play."

"What on earth's a *haiku*-play?"

"A play imbued with the spirit of *haiku*."

My master and Waverhouse, apparently

dazed by the concept of an essentially tiny poem blown out to the length of a play, say nothing; but Beauchamp presses on.

"How do you implement that interesting idea?"

"Well, since the work is of the *haiku* mode, I decided it should not be too lengthy or too viciously clear-cut. It is accordingly a one-act play; in fact a single scene."

"I understand."

"Let me first describe the setting. It must, of course, be very simple. I envisage one big willow in the center of the stage. From its trunk a single branch extends stage-right. And on that branch there's a crow."

"Won't the crow fly off?" says my master worriedly, as if talking to himself.

"That's no problem. One just ties the crow's leg to the branch with a stoutish bit of string. Now, underneath the branch there's a wooden bath-tub. And in the bath-tub, sitting sideways, there's a beautiful woman washing herself with a cotton towel."

"That's a bit decadent. Besides, who could you get to play the woman?" asks Waverhouse.

"Again, no problem. Just hire a model from an art school."

"The Metropolitan Police Bureau will undoubtedly prove sticky." My master's worriment is not allayed.

"But it ought to be all right so long as one doesn't present this work of art as some form of show. If this were the sort of thing that the police get sticky about, it would be impossible ever to draw from the nude."

"But nude models are provided for students to study, not just to stare at."

"If you scholars, the intellectual cream of Japan, remain so strait-laced in your ancient bigotry, there's no real hope for the future of Japan. What's the distinction between painting and drama? Are they not both arts?" Coldmoon, very evidently enjoying himself, lashes out at the prudery of his listeners.

"Well, let's leave all that for the moment," says Beauchamp, "but tell us how your play proceeds." He may not intend to use the play, but he clearly wants to know how that promising opening scene will be developed.

"Enter the *haiku*-poet Takahama Kyoshi. He advances along the ramp leading to the stage carrying a walking-stick and wearing a white pith-helmet. Under his silk-gauze surcoat, his white kimono, patterned with colored splashes, is tucked up at the back; and he wears shoes in the Western style. He is thus costumed to look like a contractor of Army supplies but, being a *haiku*-poet, he must walk in a leisurely manner looking as though deeply absorbed in the composition of a poem. When he reaches the main stage he notices first the willow tree and then the light-skinned lady in her bath. Startled, he looks up and sees the crow peering down at her from its long branch. At this point the poet strikes a pose, which should be held for at least fifty seconds, to indicate how deeply he is moved by the refined *haiku*-like effect of the scene before him. Then in a deep resonant voice he declaims:

> A crow
> Is in love
> With a woman in a bath

As soon as the last word has been spoken, the clappers are clacked and the curtain falls. Well now, what do you think of it? Don't you like it? I need hardly say that any sensible man would rather play the part of a *haiku*-poet than that of a high-class tart."

Beauchamp, however, looks undecided and comments with a serious face "It seems too short. I think it needs a little more action, something that will add real human interest."

Waverhouse, who has so far been keeping comparatively quiet, can hardly be expected indefinitely to pass up such a splendid opportunity for the display of his peculiar talents. "So that wee bit of a thing is what you call a *haiku*-play? Quite awful! Ueda Bin is constantly pointing out in his essays and articles that the spirit of *haiku,* as also indeed the comic spirit, lacks constructive positivism. He argues that they undermine the morals and hence the morale of the Japanese nation. And, as one would expect, whatever Bin points out is very much to the point. He'd have you laughed out of town if you dared risk staging such an arty-crafty bit of rubbish. In any case, it's all so uncleancut that no one could tell whether it's meant to be straight theater or burlesque. A thing so indeterminate could, in fact, be anything. Forgive me that I take the liberty of saying so, my dear Coldmoon, but I really do think you'd do better to stay in your laboratory and limit your creativity to the grinding of glass balls. You could, I'm sure, write hundreds of such plays but, since they could achieve nothing but the ruin of our nation, what would be the point?"

Coldmoon looks slightly huffed. "Do you think its effect is as demoralizing as all that? Myself, I think it's constructive, positivist, definitely yea-saying." He is seeking to vindicate something too unimportant to merit vindication. "The point is that Kyoshi actually makes the crow fall in love with the woman. His lines having that effect are, I consider, an affirmation of life; and that, I think, is very positivist."

"Now that," says Waverhouse, "is a totally new approach. A novel concept casting fresh light upon dramatic theory. We must listen with the deepest attention."

"As a bachelor of science, such an idea as that of a crow falling in love with a woman strikes me as illogical."

"Quite so."

"But this illogicality is expressed with such consummate artistry that it does not seem in the least illogical to the audience. The effect of great dramatic artistry is, in fact, to impose upon the listener a willing suspension of disbelief."

"I doubt it," says my master in tones of the deepest dubiety, but Coldmoon pays him no heed.

"You ask why the unreasonable should not sound unreasonable? Well, when I have given the psychological explanation, you will understand why. Of course, the emotion of being in love or of not being in love can only be experienced by the poet. It has nothing whatever to do with the crow. Similarly the concept of a crow in love is not a concept likely to cross the mind of a crow. In short, it is the poet himself who is in love with the woman. The moment Kyoshi clapped eyes on her he must have fallen head over heels in love. He then sees the crow sitting immobile on the branch and staring down at her. Being himself smitten with love for the lady, he assumes that the crow is similarly moved. He is, of course, mistaken, but nevertheless, indeed for that very reason, the basic idea of the play is not simply literary but positivist as well. I would in particular suggest that the manner in which the poet, while still contriving himself to appear objective and heart-free, transposes his own sentiments to become crow-sentiments is indisputably yea-saying and positivist. I ask you, gentlemen, am I not right?"

"It's a well-turned argument," says Waverhouse, "but I bet it would leave Kyoshi, if he ever heard it, distinctly taken aback. I accept that your exposition of the play is positivist but, if the play were to be staged, the audi-

ence-reaction would undoubtedly be nega-
tive. Don't you agree, Beauchamp?"

"Yes, I confess I think it's a little too nega-
tive." Beauchamp confesses with due critical
gravity.

My master seems to think things have gone
far enough and, to ease the pressure upon his
favorite disciple, he seeks to lead the conversation away from Coldmoon's ill-received
venture into the literary field. "But tell me,
Beauchamp," he says, "have you perhaps
written any new masterpieces recently?"

"Nothing really worth showing you, but I
am in fact thinking of publishing a collection
of them. Luckily, I chance to have the manu-
script with me, and I'd welcome your opinion
of these trifles I've composed." He thereupon
produced from his breast a package wrapped
in a cloth of purple crêpe. Loosening the
material, he carefully extracted a notebook
some fifty or sixty pages thick which he proceeded to deposit, reverently, before my
master. My master assumes his most magis-
terial mien and then, with a grave "Allow
me," opens the book. There, on the first page,
stands an inscription:

Dedicated
To the frail Opula

My master stared at the page, wordless and
with an enigmatic expression on his face, for
such a long time that Waverhouse peered
across from beside him.

"What have we here? New-style poetry? Aha! Already dedicated! How splendid of you, Beauchamp," he says with all the enthusiasm of a hound on the scent, "to come out bang with so bold a dedication. To, if my eyes do not deceive me, a certain Opula?"

My master, now looking more puzzled than enigmatic, turns to the poet. "My dear Beauchamp," he says, "this Opula, is she a real person?"

"Oh yes indeed. She's one of the young ladies whom I invited to our last Reading Party, the one where Waverhouse so generously applauded me. She lives, in fact, in this neighborhood. Actually, I called at her home on my way here but learnt, to my sorrow, that she's been away since last month. I gather that the whole family is spending the summer at Oiso." Beauchamp looks peculiarly solemn as, with corroborative detail, he affirms the reality of his dedication.

"Come now, Sneaze, don't go pulling a long face like that. This is the twentieth century and you'd best get used to it. Let's get down to considering the masterpiece. First of all, Beauchamp, this dedication seems a bit of a bosh shot. What do you mean by 'frail'?"

"Well, I meant 'frail' in the romantic sense, to convey the idea of a person infinitely delicate, infinitely refined and ethereal."

"Did you now. Well, the word can, of course, be so used but it does have other, coarser connotations. Especially if it were read as an adjectival noun, you could be thought to be calling her some sort of franion. So if I were you, I'd rephrase it."

"Could you suggest how? I'd like it to be unmisinterpretably poetic."

"Well, I think I'd say something like 'Dedicated to all that's frail beneath the nares of Opula.' It wouldn't involve much change in wording, but yet it makes an enormous difference in the feeling."

"I see," says Beauchamp. While it is quite clear that he doesn't understand the balderdash proposed by Waverhouse, he is trying hard to look as though he had grasped, considered and accepted it.

My master, who has been sitting silently, turns the first page and begins to read aloud from the opening section.

"In the fragrance of that incense which
    I burn
When I am weary, seemingly
Your soul trails in the smoky twist
    and turn
Of love requited. Woe, ah woe is me,
Who in a world as bitter as is this
Must in a mist of useless yearning
    yearn
For the sweet fire of your impassioned
    kiss.

"This, I'm afraid," he says with a sigh, "is a bit beyond me"; and he passes the notebook along to Waverhouse.

"The effect is strained, the imagery too heightened," says Waverhouse passing it on to Coldmoon.

"I . . . s . . . e . . . e," says Coldmoon, and returns it to the author.

"It's only natural that you should fail to understand it." Beauchamp leaps to his own defense. "In the last ten years the world of poetry has advanced and altered out of all recognition. Modern poetry is not easy. You can't understand it if you do no more than glance through it in bed or while you're waiting at a railway-station. More often than not, modern poets are unable to answer even the simplest questions about their own work. Such poets write by direct inspiration, and are not to be held responsible for more than the writing. Annotation, critical commentary and exegesis, all these may be left to the scholars. We poets are not to be bothered with such trivia. Only the other day some fellow with a name like Sōseki published a short-story entitled 'A Single Night.' But it's so vague that no one could make head or tail of it. I eventually got hold of the man and questioned him very seriously about the real meaning of his story. He not only refused to give any explanation but even implied that, if the story happened in fact to have any meaning at all, he couldn't care less. His attitude was, I think, typical of a modern poet."

"He may be a poet, but he sounds, doesn't he, downright odd," observes my master.

"He's a fool." Waverhouse demolishes this Sōseki in one curt breath.

Beauchamp, however, has by no means finished defending the merits of his own daft poem. "Nobody in our poetry-group is in any way associated with this Sōseki fellow, and it would be unreasonable if you gentlemen were to condemn my poems by reason of some such imagined association. I took great pains with the construction of this work, and I would like in particular to draw your attention to my telling contrast of this bitter world with the sweetness of a kiss."

"The pains you must have taken," says my master somewhat ambiguously, "have not gone unremarked."

"Indeed," says Waverhouse, "the skill with which you have made 'bitter' and 'sweet' reflect each other is as interesting as if you had spiced each syllable of a *haiku* with seventeen different peppery tastes. The saying speaks of only seven such peppery tangs but, so tasteful, Beauchamp, is the concoction you've cooked up, that no saying is sufficient to say how inimitable it is and how totally lost am I in admiration of your art." Rather unkindly, Waverhouse diverts himself at the expense of an honest man. Possibly for that reason, my master suddenly got to his feet and went off into his study. Possibly not, for he quickly re-emerged with a piece of paper in his hand.

"Now that we've considered Coldmoon's

play and Beauchamp's poem, perhaps you will grant me the boon of your expert comments on this little thing here that I've written." My master looks as if he means what he says to be taken seriously. If so, he is to be immediately disappointed.

"If it's that epitaph-thing for Mr. the-late-and-sainted Natural Man, I've heard it twice already. If not thrice," says Waverhouse dismissingly.

"For heaven's sake, Waverhouse, why don't you just pipe down. Now, Beauchamp, I'd like you to understand that this is not an example of my best and serious work. I wrote it just for fun, so I'm not especially proud of it. But let's just see if you like it."

"I'd be delighted to hear it."

"You too, Coldmoon. Since you're here, you might as well listen."

"Of course, but it's not long, is it?"

"Very short. I doubt," says my master quite untruthfully, "whether it contains as many as three score words and ten"; whereupon, giving no opportunity for further interruptions, he launches out upon a recital of his homespun master-work.

" 'The Spirit of Japan,' cries Japanese
      man;
    'Long may it live,' cries he
    But his cry breaks off in that kind of
      cough
    Which comes from the soul's T.B."

"What a magnificient opening," burbles Coldmoon with real enthusiasm. "The theme rises before one, immediate, undodgeable and imposing: like a mountain!"

> " 'The Spirit of Japan,' scream the
>   papers,
> Pickpockets scream it too:
> In one great jump the Japanese Spirit
> Crosses the ocean blue
> And is lectured upon in England,
> While a play on this staggering theme
> Is a huge success on the German stage.
> A huge success? A scream!"

"Splendid," says Waverhouse, letting his head fall backwards in token of his approbation. "It's even better than that epiphanic epitaph."

> "Admiral Tōgō has the Japanese Spirit,
> So has the man in the street:
> Fish-shop managers, swindlers,
>   murderers,
> None would be complete,
> None would be the men they are,
> None would be a man
> If he wasn't wrapped up like a tuppenny
>   cup
> In the Spirit of Japan"

"Please," breathes Coldmoon, "please do mention that Coldmoon has it too."

"But if you ask what this Spirit is
They give that cough and say
'The Spirit of Japan is the Japanese
    Spirit,'
Then they walk away
And when they've walked ten yards
    or so
They clear their throats of phlegm,
And that clearing sound is the Japanese
    Spirit
Manifest in them."

"Oh I like that," says Waverhouse, "that's a very well-turned phrase. Sneeze, you've got talent, real literary talent. And the next stanza?"

"Is the Spirit of Japan triangular?
Is it, do you think, a square?
Why no indeed!   As the words
    themselves
Explicitly declare,
It's an airy, fairy, spiritual thing
And things that close to God
Can't be defined in a formula
Or measured with a measuring-rod."

"It's certainly an interesting composition and most unusual in that, defying tradition, it has a strong didactic element. But don't you think it contains too many Spirits of Japan. One can have," says Beauchamp mildly, "too much of the best of things."

> "There's not one man in the whole of
> Japan
> Who has not used the phrase,
> But I have not met one user yet
> Who knows what it conveys.
> The Spirit of Japan, the Japanese
> Spirit,
> Could it conceivably be
> Nothing but another of those long-
> nosed goblins
> Only the mad can see?"

My master comes to the end of his poem and, believing it pregnant with eminently debatable material, sits back in expectation of an avalanche of comment. However, though the piece is undoubtedly that master-work for which the anthologists have been waiting, its endless Western form and its lack of clear meaning have resulted in the present audience not realizing that the recitation is over. They accordingly just sit there. For a long time. Eventually, no more verses being vouchsafed them, Coldmoon ventures "Is that all?"

My master answers with a noncommittal, I thought falsely carefree, kind of throaty grunt.

Very much contrary to my own expectations, Waverhouse failed to rise to the occasion with one of his usual flights of fantastication.

Instead, after a brief interval, he turned to my master and said "How about collecting some of your shorter pieces into a book? Then you, too, could dedicate it to someone."

"How about to you?" my master flippantly suggests.

"Not on your life," says Waverhouse very firmly. He takes out the scissors which he had earlier analyzed for the benefit of Mrs. Sneaze and begins clipping away at his fingernails.

Coldmoon turns to Beauchamp and, somewhat cautiously, enquires "Are you closely acquainted with Miss Opula Goldfield?"

"After I invited her to our Reading Party last spring, we became friends and we now see quite a lot of each other. Whenever I'm with her I feel, as it were, inspired; and even after we've parted, I still feel, at least for quite a time, such a flame alight within me that poems, both in the traditional forms and in the modern style, come singing up like steam from a kettle. I believe that this little collection contains so high a proportion of love-poems precisely because I am so deeply stirred by women and, in particular, by her. The only way I know by which to express my sincere gratitude is by dedicating this book to the source of its inspiration. I stand at the end of a long tradition inasmuch as, since time immemorial, no poet wrote fine poetry save under the inspiration of some deeply cherished woman."

"Is that indeed so?" says Coldmoon as though he had just learnt a fact of imponderable gravity: but deep behind the sober skin of his face I could see him laughing at the folly of his friend.

Even this gathering of gasbags cannot wheeze on for ever, and the pressure of their conversation is now fast whimpering down toward exhaustion. Being under no obligation to listen all day long to their endless blather, their carping and flapdoodle, I excused myself and went out into the garden in search of a praying mantis.

The sun is going down. Its reddened light, filtered through the green foliage of a sultan's parasol, flecks the ground in patches. High up on the trunk of the tree, cicadas are singing their hearts out. Tonight, perhaps, a little rain may fall.

I HAVE, of late, taken to taking exercise. To those who may sneer at me saying "What sauce, a mere cat taking exercise indeed!" I would like to address the few following words. It was not until recently that human beings, previously content to regard eating and sleeping as their only purposes in life, began to grasp the point of taking exercise. Let all mankind remember in what self-complacent idleness they used to pass their days; how passionately they once believed that impassivity of mind and body were the signs of a noble soul, and that the honor of a nobleman resided in his ability to do nothing more strenuous than to plant his bum on a cushion that there it might, in comfort, rot away. It is only recently that, like some infectious disease brought from the West to this pure land of the gods, a stream of silly injunctions has been sprayed upon us to take exercise, to gulp milk, to shower ourselves with freezing water, to plonk ourselves in the sea and, in the summertime, to sequester ourselves in the mountains on a diet, allegedly healthy, of nothing more solid than mist. Such importations seem to me about as

salubrious as the black plague, tuberculosis
and that very Western malady, neurasthenia.
However, since I am only one year old, born
as I was last year, I cannot personally testify
as to the state of affairs when human beings
here first began to suffer from these sicknesses.
It happened at a time before I came to float
along in this vale of tears. Nevertheless, one
may fairly equate a cat's one year with ten for
human beings: and though our span of life is
two or three times shorter than theirs, a cat
may still therein achieve full feline self-
development. It follows that any evaluation
of a cat's life and a man's life by reference to
a common time-scale must result in grievous
error.

That point is surely proven by the fact that
I, who am but a year and a few months old,
possess the discernment to make such an
analysis. In contrast, the third daughter of my
master, whom I understand to be already in
her third year, is lamentably backward, a
laggard in all learning, a slow-coach in development. Her accomplishments are limited.
She yowls, she mucks her bed and she sucks
milk from her mother. Compared with someone like myself who am distressed by the state
of the world and deplore the degeneracy of
the age, that girl is truly infantile. It is consequently not in the least surprising that I
should have stored away, deep within my
mind, the entire history of taking exercise, of
sea-bathing and of going-away-for-a-change-
of-air. If there should be anyone surprised at

a thing so trifling as this vast extent of my knowledge, it could only be another of those handicapped humans, those stumbling creatures whom heaven has retarded with the gift of no more than a measly couple of legs. From time immemorial man has been a slow-coach, so it is only very recently that such inveterate sluggards have begun to recommend the virtues of exercise, and, as if the notion were their own incredible discovery, to babble endlessly of the benefits of bobbing about in the sea. *Per contra,* I was aware of such things in my prenatal condition; and fully to realize the benisons of brine one needs but walk on a beach.

Precisely how many fish are frolicking about in so vast a volume of water, I would not care to guess; but it is certain that not a single specimen has ever fallen so sick as to need the attentions of a doctor. There they all are, swimming about in the best of health. When a fish does catch some illness, its body first becomes helpless. But let it be remembered that the death of a fish is described in Japanese as an ascension. Birds, we say, drop dead, become mere fallen things. Men are simply said to have kicked the bucket. But fish, I stress, ascend. Now, just ask anyone who's journeyed overseas, anyone who's crossed the Indian Ocean, whether they've seen a dying fish. Of course they haven't. And no wonder. However often you might plow back and forth across that endless waste of water, never would you see afloat upon its waves one single fish that had just given up its last breath. Given up, I should perhaps fish-pertinently say, its last sea-water-gulp. Had you assiduously searched since time began, were you now to go on steaming day and night up and down that wide and boundless expanse of water, not one solitary fish would ever be seen to ascend. Since fish do not ascend, their undying strength, their hardihood, indeed their deathlessness, is easily deduced.

How comes it, then, that fish should be so death-defyingly hardy? Here once again, mankind can give no answer. But the answer, as I shortly shall disclose, is simplicity itself. The answer is that fish are hardy because they incessantly bathe in the sea, because they swill salt-water. It's as simple as that. Now, since the benefits of sea-bathing are so evidenced by fish, surely it must follow that the practice would be beneficial to mankind. Lo and behold, in 1750 a certain Dr. Richard Russell came out with the humanly exaggerated pronouncement that anyone who jumped into the sea at Brighton would find that all his various diseases would be cured on the spot. Is it not laughable that it took mankind so long to arrive at so simple a conclusion? Even we cats, when the time is ripe, intend to go down to the seaside, to some place like Kamakura. But *now* is not the time. There is always a right time for everything. Just as the Japanese people before the Restoration of the Emperor both lived and died without benefit of sea-bathing, so cats today have not yet reached the appropriate stage for leaping naked into the briny deep. Timing is all-important, and a hurried job is a job half-botched. Consequently, since no cat taken today to be drowned in some shrine's canal will ever come safely home, it would be most imprudent indeed for me to go plunging in. Until by the laws of evolution we cats have developed the characteristics needed to resist the rage of overwhelming waves; until, in fact, a dead cat can be said not to have died but, like fish, to have ascended; until that happy day, I won't go near the water.

Postponing my sea-bathing to some later date, I have anyway decided to make a start on some sort of exercise. In this enlightened twentieth century, any failure to take exercise is likely to be interpreted as a sign of pauperdom. Which would be bad for one's reputation. If you don't take exercise, you will be judged incapable of taking it by reason of an inability to afford either the time or the expense; or both. It is thus no longer a simple question of not taking exercise. In olden times those who did take physical exercise, persons such as the riffraff of male servants in an upper-class household, were regarded with a proper scorn. But nowadays it is precisely those who do not take some form of physical exercise at whom the world turns up its nose. The world's evaluations of an individual's social worth, like the slits in my eyeballs, change with time and circumstance. In point of fact my pupil-slits vary but modestly between broad and narrow, but mankind's value-judgements turn somersaults and cart-wheels for no conceivable reason. Still, now that I come to think of it, there may perhaps be sense in such peculiar topsy-turvydom. For just as there are two ends to every string, there are two sides to every question. Perhaps in its extreme adaptability mankind has found a way to make apparent opposites come out with identical meanings. Thus, if one takes the symbols meaning "idea" and turns them upside-down, one finds oneself with the symbols meaning "plan." Charming, isn't it? A similar conception can be seen at work in the Japanese practice of viewing the so-called Bridge of Heaven by bending down and peering backward between one's parted legs. Seen thus, the sea and its reflection of the pine-trees on the sandbar appear like true pines reared into the sky, whereas the true pines and the sky appear as trees reflected upon the water. It is indeed a remarkable effect. Even the works of Shakespeare might be more thoroughly appreciated if they were re-examined from unorthodox positions. Someone, once in a while, should take a good long look at Hamlet through his legs. Presented upside-down, that tragedy might earn the bald remark "Ye Gods, this play is bad." How else, except by standing on their heads, can the critics in our literary world make any progress?

Considered against that background, it is

hardly surprising that those who once spoke ill of physical exercise should suddenly go crazy about sports; that even women should walk about on the streets with tennis rackets clutched in their hands. So far as I'm concerned, I have no criticisms to offer on any of these matters provided no misguided human being has the effrontery to criticize a cat for the sauciness of its interest in taking physical exercise. That said, perhaps I ought to satisfy your probable curiosity, to offer some explanation of the exercise I take.

As you are aware, it is my misfortune that my paws cannot grasp any kind of implement. I am consequently unable to pick up balls or to grip such things as bats and bloody rackets. Moreover, even could I handle them, I cannot buy them for I haven't got any money. For these two reasons, I have chosen such kinds of exercise as cost nothing and need no special equipment. I suppose you might consequently assume that my idea of exercise must be limited to merely walking about or to running away like Rickshaw Blacky with a slice of stolen tunny-fish jammed in my jaws. But to swagger about on the ground by the mere mechanical movement of four legs and in strict obedience to the laws of gravity, that is all too simple; simple and therefore totally uninteresting. There is indeed one kind of exercise called "movements" in which my master occasionally indulges. But it is, in fact, no more than its name suggests, a matter of mere mechanical movements. Which, to

my mind, is a desecration of the sanctity of
exercise. Of course, if some true incentive is
involved, I do not always scorn the simplic-
ities of mere movement. For example, I get
real pleasure from racing for dried bonito and
from going on salmon-hunts. But those
activities are related to specific objectives. If
the incentives are removed, the activities
become mere waste of spirit, ashes in the
mouth.

When there is no prize to provide the
needed stimulus, then my preference is for
exercises that demand some kind of genuine
skill. I have devised a variety of exercises
satisfying that requirement. One is jumping
from the kitchen-eaves up and onto the main
roof of the house. Another is standing with
all four legs together on the plum-blossom
shape of the narrow tile at the very top of the
roof. An especially difficult feat is walking
along the laundry-pole, which usually proves
a failure because my claws can't penetrate the
hard and slippery surface of bamboo. Perhaps
my most interesting exercise is jumping suddenly from behind onto the children's backs.
However, unless I am extremely careful about
the method and timing of such exploits, the
penalties involved can be uncommonly painful. Indeed, I derive so very little pleasure
from having my head stuffed deep in a paper-
bag that I only risk this splendid exercise
three times at most in a month. One must also
recognize the disadvantage that any success in
this form of exercise depends entirely, and

unsatisfactorily, upon the availability of some human partner. Yet another form of exercise is clawing the covers of books. In this case two kinds of snag arise. First, there is the invariable drubbing administered by my master whenever he catches me at it. Secondly, though the exercise undoubtedly develops a certain dexterity of finger, it does nothing at all for the remaining muscles of my body.

I have so far only described those comparatively crude activities which I would choose to call old-fashioned exercises. However, my newfangled sports include a few of the most exquisite refinement. First among such sports comes hunting the praying mantis, which is only less noble than hunting rats by the lesser degree of its dangers. The open season, with quarry in superb condition, runs from high mid-summer until early in the autumn. The hunt-rules are as follows. First one goes to the garden to flush one's quarry out. Given the proper weather, one may expect to find at least a brace of them browsing in the open. Next, having chosen one particular mantis, a sudden dash, a regular windslicer, is made towards the quarry. The mantis, thus alerted to its danger, rears its head and readies for the fray. For all its puniness, the mantis, at least until it realizes the hopelessness of any further resistance, is a plucky little beast; and its fatuous readiness to make a fight of it adds zest to the fun. I accordingly open by patting him lightly on the head with the flat of my right front paw.

The head is soft and is generally cocked to one side. At this point, the expression on the quarry's face adds singular edge to my pleasure. The beast is clearly puzzled. I immediately spring round behind him and, from that new position, lightly claw at his wings. These wings are normally folded carefully close but, if clawed with exactly the right degree of scratchiness, they can be harrowed loose and from beneath the beast a disheveled flurry of underwear, a yellowish tatter of stuff like thin transparent paper, droops flimsy into view. Oh what an elegant fellow! Tricked out in double-lined clothing even at the height of summer! And may it bring him luck!

Invariably at this moment the mantis twists his long green neck around to face me. Then, turning his whole body into the same direction, sometimes he defiantly advances and sometimes simply stands there like some dwarf-annoyed giraffe. If he remains transfixed in that latter attitude I shall be cheated of my exercise. Accordingly, having given him every chance to take the initiative, I then give him a stimulating smack. If the mantis happens to have the least intelligence, he will now attempt escape; but some, ill-schooled and of a barbarous ferocity, will persevere in derring-do, even to the point of launching an attack. When dealing with such savages, I carefully calculate the precisely proper moment to strike back and then, suddenly, deliver a really heavy blow as he advances at me. I would say that on such occasions the beast is usually batted sideways for a distance of between two and three feet. However, if my quarry displays a civilized recognition of its plight and drags away in pitiful retreat, then I am moved to pity. Off I go, racing along like a flying bird, two or three times around a convenient tree in the garden. Yet when I return I rarely find that the mantis has managed to crawl away more than five or six inches. Now conscious of my power, he has no stomach for continued battle. He staggers away, tottering first left and then right in dazed attempts to escape me. Matching his movements, this way and that, I harry him back and forth. Sometimes in his ultimate despair, he makes the ultimate effort of fluttering his wings. It is the nature of the wings, as of the neck, of a praying mantis to be exceedingly long and exceedingly slender. Indeed I understand that these wings are entirely ornamental and are of no more practical use to a praying mantis than are, to a human being, the English, French and German languages. It follows that, however ultimate his effort, however grand his pitiful remonstrance, no fluttering of those ineffectual wings can have on me the very least effect. One speaks of his effort but, in reality, there's nothing so purposeful about it. One should not use a word so energetic to describe the shambling totter, torn wings a-drag along the ground, of this pathetic creature. For I confess that I really do feel a wee mite sorry for my miserable antagonist. However, my need for physical exercise outweighs all other considerations, and into every life, even that of a mantis, a little rain must fall. My conscience salved, I dart beyond him from behind, twist and so confront him. In his condition, having committed himself to forward movement, he has no choice but to keep coming. Equally naturally, faced with such aggression, I have no choice but to give him a whack on the nose. My foe collapses, falls down flat with his wings spread out on either side. Extending a front paw, I hold him down in that squashed-face position whilst I take a little breather. Myself at ease again, I let the wretched perisher get up and struggle on. Then again I catch him. My strategy is based, of course, on the classic Chinese methods of Kung Ming, that military marvel of the Shu Kingdom in the third century, who, seven times in succession, first caught, then freed, his enemy. For maybe thirty minutes I pursue that classic alternation. Eventually, the mantis abandons hope and, even when free to drag himself away, lies there motionless. I lift him lightly in my mouth and spit him out again. Since, even then, he just lies loafing on the ground, I prod him with my paw. Under that stimulus the mantis hauls himself erect and makes a kind of clumsy leap for freedom. So once again down comes my quick immobilizing paw. In the end, bored by the repetitions, I conclude my exercise by eating him. Incidentally, for the benefit of those who've never munched mantis, I would report that the taste is rather unpleasant and I have been led to understand that the nutrimental value is negligible.

Next to mantis-hunting, my favorite sport is cricketing. In exactly the same way as, among the varieties of man, one can find oily creatures, cheeky chaps and chatterboxes, so among the species of cicada there are oily-cicadas, pert cicadas and chatterboxes too. The oily ones are not much fun, being in fact too greasily importunate. The cheeky chaps annoy one, being a sight too uppity. And I am consequently most interested in silencing the chatterboxes. They do not appear until the end of summer. There comes a day when, unexpectedly, the first cool wind of autumn blows through the gaps torn in the sleeves of one's kimono, making one feel a sniffling cold is surely on its way. Just about then the chatterboxes, tails cocked up behind them, start their singing din. And a deal of din they make. So much noise, in fact, one could almost believe they have no purposes in life except to chatter at the top of their rowdy voices and to be caught by cats. It is in early autumn that I catch them, and cricketing is what I call this form of taking exercise. I must first emphasize that in hunting for live chatterboxes there's no point questing on the ground. Any that are on the ground will invariably be found half-buried under ants. Those which I stalk are not the perished relics at the mercy of the pismires, but those alive and chattering away in the branches of

tall trees. Whilst I am on this general subject,
it occurs to me to query whether these noisy
creatures are shouting o-shi-i-tsuku-tsuku or
tsuku-tsuku-o-shi-i. I suspect there could be
real significance in the difference, a difference
no doubt capable of casting much-needed
light on the whole field of cicada studies. It is
a topic that cries out for the exercise of the
particular gifts of humankind. Indeed, man's
natural proclivity for this kind of investigation is the sole characteristic by which he is
superior to a cat. Which is, of course, precisely the reason that human beings, proud of
their singularity, attach so much importance
to such pettifogging points. Consequently, if
men can't offer an immediate answer, I
suggest that for all our sakes they think the
matter over very carefully. Of course, so far
as my cricketing is concerned, the outcome of
their ponderings, whatever that may be, could
hardly matter less.

Now, with respect to the practice of cricketing, all I have to do is to climb toward the
source of noise and catch the so-called singer
while he is totally absorbed in his so-called
act of singing. Superficially the simplest of all
exercises, it is in fact quite difficult. Since I
have four legs, I do not regard myself as
inferior to any other animal in the matter of
moving about on the surface of this planet.
Indeed, by mathematical deduction of comparative mobility by reference to the number
of legs involved, the average cat would seem
to be at least twice as nimble as the average

man. But when it comes to climbing trees, there are many animals more dexterous than the cat. Apart from monkeys, those absolute professionals, one is bound to concede that men, descended as they are from tree-conditioned apes, sometimes display a truly formidable skill at climbing trees. I hasten to add that, since climbing trees is unnatural, being a direct defiance of the laws of gravity, I cannot consider a failure to shine in such unreasonable activity as in any way shameful. But it is a disadvantage to a cricketer. Luckily, I happen to possess this useful set of claws which makes it possible for me, however clumsily, to get up trees: but it's not as easy as you might think. What's more, a chatterbox, unlike the pitiable mantis, really can fly. And once it takes to the wing, all my painful climbing profits me nothing. Indeed a dismal outcome. It has, moreover, the dangerous and ugly habit of pissing in one's eye. One can't complain of its taking flight in flight, but such filthy micturition is hardly playing the game. What psychological pressure induces this incontinence at the moment immediately prior to an act of aviation? Is it, perhaps, that the thought of flying is too unbearable to bear? Or is it simply that a pissed-on prowler is so shockedly surprised that his intended prey gains ample time to escape? If that latter hypothesis is correct, this urinating insect falls into a common category with the ink-ejecting squid, with the tattoo-flashing brawler in the alleyways of

Tokyo and with my poor old idiot master spouting clouds of protective Latin. Again I would stress that this question of urination at take-off is no mere piddling matter, but an issue of possibly fundamental relevance to the study of cicadas. The problem certainly merits the detailed study of a doctoral dissertation. But I digress too far. Let us return to the practicalities of cricketing.

The spot where the cicadas most thickly concentrate (if you object to my use in this context of the word "concentrate," then I was originally prepared to substitute the word "assemble," but I find that latter word so banal that I have decided to stick to "concentrate") is the green paulownia, the so-called Sultan's Parasol which, I am reliably informed, is known to the Chinese as the Chinese Parasol. Now the green paulownia is densely foliaged and each of its leaves is as big as a big round fan. It is consequently hard to see the branches where my quarry lurks; a fact which constitutes another hazard for the keen cricketer. I sometimes think that it was with my predicament in mind that the author of that popular song wrote those words of yearning for "one, though heard, invisible." At all events, the best I can do is to work my way toward that place from which the song appears to emanate.

About six feet up from the ground, the trunks of all green paulownias fork conveniently into two. Within that crotch I rest from the exertion of my initial climb and, peering upward between the backs of the leaves, try to see where the chatterboxes are. Sometimes, however, before I even get to the crotch, one or two of my potential victims grow alarmed and, with a curious rustling sound, impatiently take flight. Then I've really had it. For, judging them by their readiness to be led and their mindless passion for conformity of conduct, these chatterboxes are no less imbecile than men. As soon as the first one flies away, all the others follow. There are occasions, therefore, when by the time I've reached the fork, the whole tree stands deserted in a dead dispiriting silence. On one such day I'd climbed up to the fork only to find, however hard I peered and however much I pricked my ears, no faintest sign or sound of a chatterbox. Deciding it would be too much of a bore to start all over again in some other tree, I concluded that the sensible thing would be to stay where I was, enjoy the relaxation and wait for a second chance when the refugees returned. Before long I grew sleepy, and soon was happily far away in the pleasant land of Nod. My awakening was unpleasant, for I'd fallen thuddingly down onto a flagstone in the garden.

Nevertheless, I usually manage to catch one chatterbox for every tree I climb. It is, alas, an unavoidable characteristic of this sport, one which sadly reduces my interest in it, that, so long as I'm up in the tree, I have to hold my captive in my mouth; for, by the time I've descended and can spit him out on the ground, he is usually dead. However hard I may thereafter play with him and scratch him, he offers no response. The most exquisite moment in cricketing occurs when, after sneaking quietly up on a chatterbox whose whole vibrating being is concentrated upon song, upon the soul-absorbing business of scraping his tail-parts in and out of the main shell of his body, suddenly I pounce and my paws clamp down upon him. How piercingly he shrieks, with what a threshing ecstasy of terror he shakes his thin transparent wings in efforts to escape. The sheer speed and intensity of these happenings creates an aesthetic experience impossible to describe. One can only say that the magnificence of its death-throes is the supreme achievment of a cicada's life. Every time I catch a chatterbox I ask, in suitably pressing terms, for a demonstration of his thrilling artistry. When tired of his performance, I beg his pardon for the interruption and pop him into my mouth. Occasional virtuosi have been known to continue with their act even after my mouth has closed behind them.

After cricketing, my next most favored form of physical exercise is pine-sliding. A detailed explanation would be too much, so I'll offer only the minimum of comment needed for an understanding of this sport. Its name suggests that it involves sliding down pine-trees, but in fact it doesn't. It is, indeed, another form of climbing trees. But whereas when cricketing I climb to catch a chatterbox, when pine-sliding I climb purely for the climbing. Ever since Genzaemon warmed the room for Lay-priest Saimyoji, that one-time Regent at Kamakura, by burning those trees to which Genzaemon in his own happier days had been particularly attached, the pine-tree has been not only, as the song about that incident assures us, naturally an evergreen but also most unnaturally rough-barked to one's touch. Whatever the explanation, there is certainly no tree less slippery than the pine, and no trunk in the world affords a better climbing surface either for hands or for feet. Clearly, when it comes to claws, nothing is more clawable and I can consequently run up a pine-trunk in one breath.

Having run up, I run down. Now there are two styles of downward running. One way is to descend, effectively upside down, with one's head facing the ground; and the other is to descend tail-first in the normal attitude for an ascending climb. And which, I would ask you know-all human beings, would you suppose is the more difficult style of the two? Being but shallow-brained, you probably think that one would find it easier to position one's head so as to lead in the direction of desired movement; and you'd be wrong. When you heard me speak of running downward, no doubt you thought immediately of Yoshitsune's headlong horse-charge down the cliff at Hiyodori-goe; and I can imagine you thinking to yourself that anything good enough for a human hero like Yoshitsune must be more than sufficient for some unnamed unknown cat. But such disdain would be entirely misplaced. Just to begin with, do you know how cats' claws grow, their directional positioning in accordance with their function? They are, in fact, retrorsely curved so that, like firemen's hooks, they are peculiarly suited to catching hold of things and drawing them chestward. They are virtually useless for pushing things away. Now, since I am a terrestrial creature, it would be a breach of natural law if, having dashed up a pine-tree trunk, I were to remain indefinitely and unsupported at the swaying top of the tree. I would certainly fall down. And, if that fall were nowise checked, the rate of my descent could well prove lethal. Thus, when I take measures to mitigate the potentially disastrous effects of the laws of gravity and nature, I call the consequent process of descent "descending." Though there may seem to be a substantial difference between descending and free-falling, it isn't as great as one might fondly imagine; indeed, no more than a single letter's worth. Since I do not care to free-fall out of a pine-tree-top, I needs must find some means to check the natural acceleration of my body. And that's where my claws come in; or rather, out. Being retrorsely curved, all my twenty claws, appropriately extended from my heaven-facing body, provide a gripping-power and frictional resistance sufficient to transform the hazards of free-fall into the relative safety of descent. Simple, isn't it? But you just try to come down from a pine-tree like a wolf on the fold in the headlong Yoshitsune style, and that's not simple at all. Claws are useless. Nothing retards the slithering acceleration of your body's weight, and those who'd hoped thus safely to descend finish up by plummeting earthward like boulders dropped by rocs. You will accordingly appreciate that the headlong descent of Hiyodori-goe was an exceptionally difficult feat, one which only a veritable hero could successfully accomplish. Among cats, probably only I, the Yoshitsune of my kind, can pull it off. I accordingly feel I have earned my right to give a name to this particular sport, and I have chosen "pine-sliding."

I cannot conclude these few words on the subject of sport without at least some mention of "going round the fence." My master's garden, rectangular in shape, is on all sides separated from neighboring properties by a bamboo fence about three feet high. The section running parallel to the veranda is some fifty feet long, and the two side-sections are each about half that length. The object of the aforementioned sport is to walk right round the whole property without falling off the thin top-edge of the fence. There are times, I confess, when I do topple off; but, when successful, I find such tours of the horizon eminently gratifying. Really, great fun. The fence is supported here and there, and particularly at the corners, by sturdy cedar-stakes fire-hardened at each end, on the tops of which I can conveniently take breathers in the course of my circumambulation. I found myself today in really rather good form. Before lunch I managed three successful tours, and on each occasion my performance improved. Naturally, every improvement adds to the fun. I was just about halfway home on my fourth time round when three crows, gliding down from the next-door roof, settled on the fence-top, side by side, some six short feet ahead of me. Cheeky bastards! Quite apart from the fact that they're interrupting my exercise, such low-born ill-bred rain-guttersnipes have no right whatever to come trespassing, indeed seemingly to start squatting, on my fence-property. So I told them, in terms of hissing clarity, to get lost. The nearest crow, turning its head toward me, appears to be grinning like a half-wit. The next one unconcernedly studies my master's garden. And the third continues wiping his filthy beak on a projecting splinter of the fence-bamboo. He had all too evidently just finished eating something rather nasty. I stood there balanced on the fence, giving them a civilized three minutes' grace to shove off. I've heard that these birds are commonly called Crow-magnons, and they certainly look as daft and primitively barbarous as their uncouth nick-name would suggest. Despite my courteous waiting, they neither greeted me nor flew away. Becoming at last impatient, I began slowly to advance; whereupon the nearest Crowmagnon tentatively stirred his wings. I thought he was at last backing off in face of my power, but all he did was to shift his posture so as to present his arse rather than his head toward me. Outright insolence! Conduct unbecoming even a Crowmagnon. Were we on the ground, I would call him to immediate account; but, alas, being as I am engaged upon a passage both strenuous and perilous, I really can't be bothered to be diverted from my purpose by such aboriginal naiseries. On the other hand, I do not greatly care for the idea of being stuck here while a trey of brainless birds waits for whatever impulse will lift them into the air. For one thing, there's my poor tired feet. Those feathered lightweights are used to standing around in such precarious places so that, if my fence-top happens to please them, they might perch here forever. I, on the other hand, am already exhausted. This is my fourth time round today, and this particular exercise is anyway no less tricky than tight-rope-walking. At the best of times, each teetering step I take could throw me clean off-balance, which makes it all the more un-pardonable that these three blackamoors should loaf here blocking the way. If it comes to the worst, I shall just have to abandon today's exercises and hop down from the fence. It's a bore, of course, but perhaps I might as well hop down now. After all, I am heavily outnumbered by the enemy. Besides, the poor simple things do seem to be strangers in these parts. Their beaks, I notice, are al-

most affectedly pointed, the sort of savage,
stabbing snout that, found amongst his sons, would make its foul possessor the most sharply favored member of a long-nosed goblin's brood. The signs are unmistakable that these Crowmagnon louts will be equally ill-natured. If I start a fight and then, by sheer mischance, happen to lose my footing, the loss of face will be much greater than if I just chose to disengage. Consequently thinking that it might be prudent to avoid a showdown, I had just decided to hop down when the arse-presenting savage offered me a rudery. "Arseholes," he observed. His immediate neighbor repeated this coarse remark, while the last one of the trio took the trouble to say it twice. I simply could not overlook behavior so offensive. First and foremost, to allow myself to be grossly insulted in my own garden by these mere crows would reflect adversely upon my good name. Should you object that I do not have a name to be reflected upon, I will amend that sentence to refer to reflections upon my honor. When my honor is involved, cost what it may, I cannot retreat. At this point it occurred to me that a disorderly rabble is often described as a "flock of crows"; so it is just possible that, though they outnumber me three to one, when it comes to the crunch they'll prove more weak than they look. Thus comforted, thus grimly resolute, I began slowly to advance. The crows, oblivious to my action, seem to be talking among them-

selves. They *are* exasperating! If only the
fence were wider by five or six inches, I'd
really give them hell. But as things are, however vehemently vexed I may feel, I can only
tiptoe slowly forward to avenge my injured
honor. Eventually I reached a point a bare
half-foot away from the nearest bird and was
urging myself onward to one last final effort
when, all together and as though by pre-
arrangement, the three brutes suddenly
flapped their wings and lumbered up to hang
a couple of feet above me in the air. The
down-draught gusted into my face. Unsport-
ingly surprised, I lost my balance and fell off
sideways into the garden.

Kicking myself for permitting such a
shameful mishap to occur, I looked up from
the ground to find all three marauders safely
landed back again where they had perched
before. Their three sharp beaks in parallel
alignment, they peer down superciliously into
my angry eyes. The bloody nerve of them! I
responded with a glowering scowl. Which
left them quite unmoved. So next I snarled
and arched my back. Equally ineffective. Just
as the subtlety of symbolic poetry is lost on a
materialist, so were the symbols of my anger
quite meaningless to the crows. Which, now
that I reflect upon the matter, is perfectly
understandable. Hitherto, and wrongly, I
have been seeking to cope with crows as if
they had been cats. Had that been the case,
they would by now most certainly have
reacted. But crows are crows, and what but

crow-behavior can anyone expect of them? My efforts have, in fact, all been as pointless as the increasingly short-tempered arguments of a businessman trying to budge my master; as pointless as Yoritomo's gift of a solid silver cat to the unworldly Saigyo; as pointless as the bird-shit that these fools and their fool cousins fly over to Ueno to deposit on the statue of poor Saigo Takamori. Once I have conceived a thought, I waste no time before I act upon it. It were better to give up than to persist in a dialogue with dunces, so I abandoned my endeavors and withdrew to the veranda.

It was time for dinner anyway.

Exercise has merits, but one mustn't overdo it. My whole body felt limp and almost slovenly. What's more I feel horribly hot. We are now at the beginning of autumn, and during my exercise my fur seems to have become saturated with afternoon sunshine. The sweat which oozes from the pores in my skin refuses to drop away but clings in greasy clots around the roots of every separate hair. My back itches. One can clearly distinguish between itches caused by perspiration and itches caused by creeping fleas. If the site of the itch lies within reach of my mouth, I can bite the cause, and if within reach of my feet, I know precisely how to scratch it; but if the irritation is at the midpoint of my spine, I simply can't get at it. In such a case, one must either frot oneself on the first available human being or scrape one's back against a pine-tree's bark. Since men are both vain and stupid, I approach them in a suitably ingratiating manner using, as they would say, "tones that would wheedle a cat." Such are the tones men sometimes use to me; but, seen from my position, the phrase should be "tones by which a cat may be wheedled." Not that it matters. Anyway, human beings being the nitwits that they are, a purring approach to any of them, either male or female, is usually interpreted as proof that I love them; and they consequently let me do as I like, and on occasions, poor dumb creatures, they even stroke my head. Of late, however, just because some kind of parasitic insect, fleas, in fact, have taken to breeding in my fur, even my most tentative approaches to a human being evoke a gross response. I am grabbed by the scruff of the neck and pitched clean out of the room. It seems that this sudden aversion stems from human disgust with those barely visible and totally insignificant insects which I harbor. A heartless and most callous attitude! How can such inconsiderate behavior possibly be justified by the presence in my coat of one or two thousand footling fleas? The answer is, of course, that Article One of those Laws of Love (by which all human creatures regulate their lives) specifically enjoins that "ye shall love one another for so long as it serves thine individual interest."

Now that the human attitude towards me has so completely changed, I cannot exploit manpower to ease my itching however virulent it may become. I therefore have no choice but to resort to the alternative method of finding relief in scraping myself on pine-bark. To that end I was just going down the veranda-steps when I realized that even this alternative solution was a silly idea and would not work. The point is that pines secrete an extremely sticky resin which, once it has gummed the ends of my fur together, cannot be loosened even if struck by lightning or fired upon by the whole Russian Baltic Fleet. What's more, as soon as five hairs stick together, then ten, then thirty hairs get inextricably stuck. I am a dainty cat of candid temperament, and any creature as clinging, poisonous and vindictive as this tenacious resin is an anathema to me. I cannot stand persons of that kind; and even if one such particular person were the most beautiful cat in the world, let alone a creature loathsome as resin, still I'd be revolted. It is outrageous that my charmingly pale gray coat can be ruined by a substance whose social and evolutionary status is no higher than that of the gummy muck which streams in the cold north wind from the corners of Rickshaw Blacky's eyes. Resin ought to realize the impropriety of its nature, but will, of course, do no such thing. Indeed, the very moment my back makes contact with a pine-tree, great clots of resin gather on my fur. To have anything to do with so insensitive, so inconsiderate a creature would not only be beneath my personal dignity but would be a defilement to anyone in my coat and lineage. I conclude that, however fleasome I may feel, I have no choice but to grin and bear it. Nonetheless, it is extremely disheartening to find that the two standard means of alleviating my discomfort are both unavailable. Unless I can quickly find some other solution, the irritation in my skin and the thought of gumminess in my mind will bring me to a nervous breakdown.

Sinking down upon my hind-legs into a thinking posture, I had scarcely begun my search for bright ideas when an illuminating memory flashed upon me. Every so often my scruffy master saunters off out of the house with a cake of soap and a hand-towel. When he returns some thirty or forty minutes later, his normally dull complexion, while not exactly glowing, has nevertheless acquired a certain modest liveliness. If such expeditions can confer a sheen of vitality upon that shabby sloven, what wonders they might work upon myself. It is, of course, true that I am already so extremely handsome that improvements, if possible, are hardly necessary; but if by some misfortune I were to fall sick and perish at this very tender age of one year and a few odd months, I could never forgive myself for allowing so irremediable a loss to be inflicted upon the populace of the world. I believe that the object of my master's sorties is one of those devices invented by mankind as a means of easing the tedium of its existence. Inasmuch as the public bath is an invention of mankind, it can hardly be much use to anyone but, clutching as I am at straws, I might as well investigate the matter. If it's as pointless as I anticipate, nothing would be simpler than to drop my enquiries; but I remain unsure whether human beings are sufficiently broad-minded to give a cat, a member of another species, even a chance to investigate the efficacy of an institution devised for human purposes. I cannot imagine that I could be refused entry when nobody dreams of questioning the casual comings and goings of my master, but it would be socially most embarrassing to find myself turned from the door. Prudence suggests the wisdom of reconnaissance and, if I like the look of the place, then I can hop in with a hand-towel in my mouth. My plan of action formed, I set off for the public bath at a properly leisurely pace.

As one turns left around the corner from our side-street, one may observe a little further up the road an object like an upended bamboo waterpipe puffing thin smoke-fumes straight up into the sky. That fuming finger marks the site of the public bathhouse. I stole in through its back entrance. That style of entry is usually looked down upon as mean-spirited or cowardly, but such criticisms are merely the tedious grumbles spiced with jealousy which one must expect from persons only capable of gaining access by front doors. It is abundantly clear from the records of history that persons of high intelligence invariably launch attacks both suddenly and from the rear. Furthermore, I note from my study of *The Making of a Gentleman* (volume two, chapter one, pages five and six) that a back-door, like a gentleman's last will and testament, provides the means whereby an individual establishes his true moral excellence. Being a truly twentieth-century cat, I have had included in my education more than sufficient of such weighty learning to make it inappropriate for anyone to sneer at my selected mode of entry. Anyway, once I was inside, I found on my immediate left a positive mountain of pine-logs cut into eight-inch lengths and, next to it, a heaped-up hill of coal. Some of my readers may wonder what the subtle significance of my careful distinction between a mountain of logs and a mere hill of coal is. There is, in fact, no subtle significance whatever. I simply used the two words, "hill" and "mountain," as they should correctly be used. Far from having time to think about literary niceties, I am overwhelmed with pity for the human race which, having regularly dieted on such revolting objects as rice, birds, fish and even animals, is now apparently reduced to munching lumps of coal. Right in front of me I see an open entrance about six feet wide. I peep through and find everything dead quiet but, from somewhere beyond, there comes a lively buzz of human voices and I deduce that the bath must be where the sound originates. I move forward between the wood-pile and the coal-heap, turn left and find a glazed window to my right. On the ledge below, a considerable number of small round tubs is piled up into a pyramid. My heart goes out to them, for it must be painfully contrary to a round thing's concept of reality to be constricted within a triangular world. To the south of these pails the sill juts out for a few feet with, as if to welcome me, wooden boarding on it. Since the board is roughly three feet up from the ground, it is, from my point of view, at an ideal hopping-height. "All right," I said to myself; and, as I flew up nimbly to the board, the public bath, like something dangled, suddenly appeared beneath my very nose.

There is nothing in the world more pleasant than to eat something one has never yet eaten or to see something one has never seen before. If my readers, like my master, spend thirty or forty minutes on three days of every passing week in the world of the public bath, then of course that world can offer them few surprises: but if, like me, they have never seen that spectacle, they should make immediate arrangements to do so. Don't worry about the deathbed of your parents, but at all costs do not miss the grand show of the public bath. The world is wide, but in my opinion it has no sight more startlingly remarkable to offer.

Wherein, you ask, resides its crass spectacularity? Well, it is so variously spectacular that I hesitate to particularize. First of all, the human beings vociferously swarming about beyond the window-glass are all stark-naked. As totally unclothed as Formosan aborigines.

Primeval Adams still prancing about in this twentieth century. I am moved by so much nudity to preface my comments with a history of clothing; but it would take so long that I will spare my readers any rehash of the learned observations of Herr Doktor Diogenes Teufelsdrockh in his monumental study on this subject *(Die Kleider, Werden und Wizken)* and simply refer them to a slightly less learned commentary on that work, Mr. Thomas Carlyle's *Sartor Resartus.* The essential fact remains that the clothes are the man, that the ungarbed man is nothing. Skipping centuries of sartorial civilization, indeed a tautological phrase, I would remind my readers that Beau Nash, in the heyday of his social regulation of eighteenth-century Bath, a royally patronized hot-springs spa in the west of England, established the inflexible rule that men and women submerging themselves in those salutary waters should nevertheless be clothed from their shoulders down to their feet. A further relevant incident occurred, again in a certain English city, just after the mid-point of the nineteenth century. It so happened that this city then founded a School of Art and, quite naturally, the school's function involved the presence and display of various studies, drawings, paintings, models and statues of the naked human figure. But the inauguration of this school placed both its own staff and the city fathers in a deeply embarrassing situation. There could be no question but that the

leading ladies of the city must be invited to
the opening ceremony. Unfortunately, all
civilized females of that era were unshakably
sure that human beings are clothes-animals
having no relationship whatever, let alone
blood-kinship, with the skin-clad apes. A
man without his clothes, they knew it for a
fact, was like an elephant shorn of its trunk,
a school without its students, soldiers devoid
of courage. Any one without the other
of these pairs would be so totally de-char-
acterized as to become, if not a complete
nonentity, at least an entity of a basely tran-
substantiated nature; and a man so tran-
substantiated would be, at best, a beast. The
ladies, as the saying is, laid it on the line.
"For us to consort with such beast-humans,
even though those bestialities were only
present in the form of drawings and statues,
would compromise our honor. If they are to
be present at the ceremony, we will not
attend." The school authorities thought the
ladies were all being a little silly but, in the
West as in the East, women, however phys-
ically unfit for the hard slog of pounding
rice or of slashing about on the battlefield,
are indispensably ornamental features of any
opening ceremony. What, then, could be
done? The school authorities took themselves
off to a draper's shop, bought thirty-five and
seven-eighths rolls of suitable black material
and clothed their beastly prints, their less-
than-human statues, in a hundred yards of
humanizing huckaback. Lest any lady's

modesty might be outraged accidentally, they even masked the faces of their statues in swathes of sable stuffs. European marble and Hellenic plaster thus yashmaked out of the animal kingdom, I am happy to record that the ceremony went off to the complete satisfaction of all concerned.

From those remarkable accounts the importance of clothes to mankind may be deduced; but, very recently, there has been a swing in the opposite direction and people may now be found who go about incessantly advocating nudity, praising nude pictures and generally making a naked menace of themselves. I think they are in error. Indeed, since I have remained decently clothed from the moment of my birth, how could I think otherwise? The craze for the nude began when, at the Renaissance, the traditional customs of the ancient Greeks and Romans were re-popularized, for their own lewd ends, by the Italianate promoters of that cultural rebirth. The ancient Greeks and Romans were culturally accustomed to nudity, and it is highly unlikely that they recognized any connection between nakedness and public morality. But in northern Europe the prevailing climate is cold. Even in Japan there is a saying that "one cannot travel naked," so that, by natural law, in Germany or England, a naked man is very soon a dead one. Since dying is daft, northerners wear clothes. And when everyone wears clothes, human beings become clothes-animals. And having once become clothes-animals, they are unable to conceive that any naked animal whom they may happen to run across could possibly also be human. Its absence of clobber immediately identifies its brutish nature. Consequently, it is understandable that Europeans, especially northern Europeans, might regard nude pictures and nude statues as essentially bestial. In other words, Europeans and Japanese have the good sense to recognize nudes and representations of nudity as life-forms inferior to cats. But nudes are beautiful, you say? What of it? Beasts, though beautiful, are beasts. Some of my more knowledgeable readers, seeking to catch me in an inconsistency, may possibly ask whether I've ever seen a European lady in evening dress? Inevitably, being only a cat, I've never had that honor; but I am reliably advised that Western ladies in formal evening wear do in fact expose their shoulders, arms and even breasts. Which is, of course, disgusting. Before Renaissance times, women's dress-styles did not sink to such scandalous levels, to such ridiculous décolletages. Instead, at all times women wore the clothes one would normally expect on any human being. Why, then, have they transformed themselves to look like vulgar acrobats? It would be far too wearisome to set down all the dreary history of that decadence. Let it suffice that those who know the reasons, know them; and that those who don't, don't need to. At all events, whatever the historical background, the fact remains that modern women, each and every night, trick themselves out in virtual undress and evince the deepest self-satisfaction with their bizarre appearances. However, it would seem that somewhere under that beastly brazenness, they retain some spark of human feeling; because, as soon as the sun comes up, they cover their shoulders, sleeve their arms and tuck away their breasts. It is all the more odd in that, not only do they sheathe themselves by day to the point of near-invisibility, but they carry their lunacy to the extreme of considering it extremely disgraceful to expose so much as a single day-lit toenail to the public view. Such inane contrariety surely proves that women's evening dresses are the brainchild of some gibbering conference of brain-damaged freaks. If women resent that logic, why don't they try walking about in the daytime with bared shoulders, arms and breasts? The same type of enquiry should also be addressed to nudists. If they are so besotted with the nude, why don't they strip their daughters? And why, while they're about it, don't they and their families stroll around Ueno Park in no more than that nakedness they so affect to love? It can't be done, they say? But of course it can. The only reason why they hesitate is not, I bet, because it can't be done, but simply because Europeans don't do it. The proof of my point is in their dusk behavior. There they are, swaggering down to the Imperial Hotel, all dolled up in those crazy evening dresses. What origin

and history do such cockeyed costumes
have? Nothing indigenous. Our bird-brained
ladies flaunt themselves in goose-skinned
flesh and feathers solely because that is the
mode in Europe. Europeans are powerful;
so it matters not how ridiculous or daft
their goings on, everyone must imitate even
their daftest designs. Yield to the long, and
be trimmed down; yield to the powerful,
and be humbled; yield to the weighty, and be
squashed. Prudence demands a due degree of
yielding, but surely only dullards yield all
along the line, surely only chimpanzees ape
everything they see. If my readers answer that
they can't help being dullards, can't help being
born without ability to discriminate in imitation, then of course I pardon them. But in
that case, they must abandon all pretense
that the Japanese are a great nation. I might
add that all my foregoing comments apply
with equal force in the field of academic
studies; but, since I am here only concerned
with questions of clothing, I will not now
press the scholastic parallels.

I think I have established the importance
of their clothes to human beings. Indeed,
their clothing is so demonstrably all-important to them that one may reasonably wonder
whether human beings are clothes or clothes
the current acme of the evolutionary process.
I am tempted to suggest that human history
is not the history of flesh and bone and blood,
but a mere chronicle of costumes. Things have
indeed come to a pretty pass when a naked

man is seen, not as a man, but as a monster.
If by mutual agreement all men were to become monsters, obviously none would see
anything monstrous in the others. Which
would be a happy situation, were it not that
men would be unhappy with it. When mankind first appeared upon the earth, a benign
Nature manufactured them to standard
specifications and all, equally naked, were
pitched forth into the world. Had mankind
been created with an inborn readiness to be
content with equality, I cannot see why, born
naked, they should have been discontent to
live and die unclothed. However, one of these
primeval nudists seems to have communed
with himself along the following lines. "Since
I and all my fellowmen are indistinguishably
alike, what is the point of effort? However
hard I strive, I cannot of myself climb beyond
the common rut. So, since I yearn to be con-
spicuous, I think I'll drape myself in something that will draw the eyes and blow the
minds of all these clones around me." I would
guess that he thought and thought for at
least ten years before he came up with a stu-
pendous idea, that glory of man's inventiveness, pants. He put them on at once and,
puffed up with pride and all primordial pomp-
ousness, paraded about among his startled
fellows. From him descend today's quaint-
clouted rickshawmen. It seems a little strange
to have taken ten long years to think up
something as simple, and as brief, as shorts:
but the strangeness is only a kind of optical

illusion created by time's immensely long
perspective. In the days of man's remote
antiquity no such breathtaking invention as
pants had ever been achieved. I've heard that
it took Descartes, no intellectual slouch, a
full ten years to arrive at his famous conclusion, obvious surely to any three-year-old,
that I think and therefore I am. Since original
thought is thus demonstrably difficult, perhaps one should concede that it was an intellectual feat, even if it took ten years, for the
wits of proto-rickshawman to formulate the
notion of knickers. At all events, ennobled by
their knickers, the breed of rickshawmen
became lords of creation and stalked the
highways of the world with such o'erweening
pride that some of the more spirited among
the cloutless monsters were provoked into
competition. Judging by its uselessness, I
would guess that they spent a mere six years
in planning their particular invention, the
good-for-nothing surcoat. The knickers' glory
faded and the golden age of surcoats shone
upon the world; and from those innovators
are descended all the green-grocers, chemists,
drapers and haberdashers of today. When
twilight fell, first upon knickers and then
upon surcoats, there came the dawn of Japanese skirted-trousers. These were designed by
monsters peeved by the surcoat-boom, and
the descendants of their inventors include
both the warriors of medieval times and
all contemporary government officials. The
plain, if regrettable, fact is that all the orig-

inally naked monsters strove vaingloriously to outdo each other in the novelty and weirdness of their gear. The ultimate grotesquerie has only recently appeared in swallow-tailed jackets. Yet if one ponders the history of these quaint manifestations, one recognizes that there is nothing random in their occurrence. The development was neither haphazard nor aimless. On the contrary, it is man's deathless eagerness to compete, the driving stretch of his intrepid spirit, his resolute determination to outdo all other members of his species, which has guided the production of successive styles of clothing. A member of this species does not go around shouting aloud that he or she differs in himself (or herself) from others of the species. Instead each one goes about wearing different clothes. From this observed behavior a major psychological truth about this race of forked destroyers may be deduced: that, just as nature abhors a vacuum, "mankind abhors equality." Being thus psychologically determined, they now have no choice whatever but to continue enveloping themselves in clothes and would regard a deprivation thereof with as much alarm as they would face a cutting off of flesh or the removal of a bone. To them it would be absolute madness to cast their various clouts, a ripping away of their essential human substance; and as unthinkable to attempt a return to their original condition of equality. Even if they could bear the shame of being accounted lunatics, it would not be feasible to return to a state of nature in which, by all civilized standards, they would automatically become not merely lunatics but monsters. Even if all the billions of human inhabitants of this globe could be rehabilitated as monsters, even if they were purged of their shame by total reassurance that, since all were monsters, none were monsters, believe you me, it still would do no good. The very next day after the reign of equality among monsters had been re-established, the monsters would be at it once again. If they can't compete with their clothes on, then they will compete as monsters. With every man-jack stark-staring naked, they would begin to differentiate between degrees of staring starkness. For which reason alone, it would, I think, be best if clothes were not abandoned.

It is consequently incredible that the assorted human creatures now displayed before my very eyes should have taken off their clothes. Surcoats, skirted trousers, even their smallest smalls, things from which their owners would as soon be parted as from their guts and bladders, are all stacked up on shelves while the re-created monsters are, with complete composure, even chatting, scandalously exposing their archetypal nudity to the public view. Are you surprised then, gentle readers, that some time back I described this scene as genuinely spectacular? Shocked as I was, and am, it will be my honor

to record for the benefit of all truly civilized
gentlemen as much as I can of this extraordinary sight.

I must start by confessing that, faced by
such mind-boggling chaos, I don't know how
to start describing it. The monsters show no
method in their madness, and it consequently
is difficult to systematize analysis thereof. Of
course, I can't be sure that it actually is a bath,
but I make the wild surmise that it can't be
anything else. It is about three feet wide and
nine feet long, and is divided by an upright
board into two sections.

One section contains white-colored bath-
water. I understand that this is what they call
a medicated bath: it has a turbid look, as
though lime had been dissolved in it. Actually,
it looks not only turbid with lime but also
heavily charged and scummed with grease.
It's hardly a wonder that it looks so whitely
stale, for I'm told that the water is changed
but once a week. The other section comprises
the ordinary bath; but, here again, by no
stretch of the imagination could its water be
described as crystal clear or pellucid. It has
the peculiarly repulsive color of stirred
rain-water which, against the danger of fire,
has stood for months in a rain-tank on a
public street. Next, though the effort kills me,
I will describe the monsters themselves. I see
two youngsters standing beside that tank of
dirty water. They stand facing each other and
are pouring pail after pail of hot water over
each other's bellies. Which certainly seems a

worthwhile occupation. The two men are faultlessly developed, so far as the sunburnt blackness of their skin is concerned. As I watch them, thinking that these monsters have remarkably sturdy figures, one of them, pawing at his chest with a hand-towel, suddenly speaks to the other. "Kin, old man, I've got a pain right here. I wonder what it is."

"That's your stomach. Stomach pains can kill you. You'd better watch it carefully," is Kin's most earnest advice.

"But it's here, on my left," says the first one, pointing at his left lung.

"Sure, that there's your stomach. On the left, the stomach; and on the right, the lung."

"Really? I thought the stomach was about here," and this time he taps himself lightly on the hip.

"Don't be silly, that's the lumbago," Kin mockingly replies.

At this point, a man of about twenty-five or twenty-six and sporting a thin moustache jumped into the bath with a plop. Next minute, the soap and loosened dirt upon his body rose to the surface, and the water glinted richly as if it might be mined for mineral wealth. Right beside him a bald-headed old man is talking to some close-cropped crony. Only their heads are visible above the water.

"Nothing's much fun any more when you get to be old like me. Once one gets decrepit, one can't keep up with the youngsters. But when it comes to a hot bath, even though they say that only lads can take real heat, that, for me, must still be really hot. Otherwise," the old man boastfully observed, "I don't feel right."

"But you, sir, are in spanking health. Not bad at all to be as energetic as you are."

"I'm not all that energetic, you know. I only manage to keep free from illness. A man, they say, should live to be a hundred and twenty provided he does nothing bad."

"What! Does one live as long as that?"

"Of course. I guarantee it up to a hundred and twenty. In the days before the Restoration there was a family called Magaribuchi—they were personal retainers of the Shogun—they used to live up here in Tokyo at Ushigome— and one of their male servants lived to a hundred and thirty."

"That's a remarkable age."

"Yes, indeed. He was in fact so old he'd clean forgotten his age. He told me he could remember it until he turned a hundred, but then he just lost count. Anyway, when I knew him he was a hundred and thirty and still going strong. I don't know what's become of him. For all I know, he may be out there still, still alive and kicking." So saying, he emerged from the bath. His whiskered friend remained in the water, grinning to himself and scattering all around him suds that glittered like small flecks of mica. The man who thereupon got into the bath was certainly no ordinary monster; for all across his back was spread a vast tattoo. It seemed to represent that legendary hero, Iwami Jutarō, about to decapitate a python with a huge high-brandished sword. For some sad reason, the tattoo has not yet been completed and the python must be guessed at. The great Jutarō looks a mite discomfited. As this illustrated man jumped into the water, "Much too tepid," he remarked. The man entering immediately behind him seems disposed to agree. "Oh dear," he says, "they ought to hot it up a bit." Just the same his features crack into a strained grimace, as though the water were in fact too hot for him. Finding himself right next to the tattooed monster, "Hello, chief," he greets him.

The tattooed monster nodded and, after a while, enquired "And how is Mr. Tami?"

"Couldn't say. He's gone so potty about gambling. . . ."

"Not just gambling only . . ."

"So? There's something wrong with that one. He's always bloody-minded. I don't know, but no one really likes him. Can't quite put a finger on it. Somehow one can't quite trust him. A man with a trade just shouldn't be like that."

"Exactly. Mr. Tami is rather too pleased with himself. Too damn stuck up, I'd say. That's why folk don't trust him. Wouldn't you say?"

"You're right. He thinks he's in a class by himself. Which never pays."

"All the old craftsmen around here are dying off. The only ones left are you, Mr.

Moto the cooper, the master-brickmaker, and that's about it. Of course, as you know, I too was born in these parts. But just take Mr. Tami. Nobody knows where he sprang from."

"True. It's a wonder that he's come as far as he has."

"Indeed it is. Somehow nobody likes him. Nobody even wants to pass the time of day with such an awkward bastard." Poor old Mr. Tami is getting it in the neck from all and sundry.

Shifting my gaze away from the section filled with filthy rain-water, I now concentrate upon the section filled with limey goo. It proves to be packed with people. Indeed, it would be more exact to describe it as containing hot water between men than as containing men in its hot water. All the creatures here are, moreover, quite remarkably lethargic. For quite some time now, men have been climbing in but none has yet climbed out. One cannot wonder that the water gets fouled when so many people use it and a whole week trundles by before the water's changed. Duly impressed by the turmoil in that tub, I peered more deeply among its tight-squeezed monsters and there I found my wretched master cowering in the left-hand corner, squashed and parboiled poppy-red. Poor old thing! Someone ought to make a gap and let him scramble out. But no one seems willing to budge an inch, and indeed my master himself appears perfectly happy to stay where he is.

He simply stands there motionless as his skin climbs through the graduations of red to a vile vermilion. What a ghastly ordeal! I guess his readiness to suffer such dire reddening reflects a determination to extract his full two far-things' worth in return for the bathhouse fee; but, devoted as I am to that dim monster of mine, I cannot sit here comfy on my ledge without worrying lest, dizzied by steam and medicating chemicals, he drown if he dallies longer. As these thoughts drifted through my mind, the fellow floating next but one to my master frowns and then remarks "All the same, this is a bit too strong. It's boiling up, really scorching, from somewhere here behind me." I deduce that, reluctant to come out with a flat complaint which might impugn his manliness, he is trying indirectly to rouse the sympathy of his boiling fellow-monsters.

"Oh no; this is just about right. Any cooler, and a medicinal bath has no effect at all. Back where I come from we take them twice as hot as this." Some braggart speaks from the depths of swirling steam.

"Anyway, what the hell kind of good can these baths do?" enquires another monster who has covered his knobbly head with a neatly folded hand-towel.

"It's good for all sorts of things. They say it's good for everything. In fact, it's terrific," replies a man with a face one could mistake, as much by reason of its color as of its shape, for a haggard cucumber. I thought to myself that if these limey waves are truly so effective, he ought at least to look a little more plump, a little more firm on the vine.

"I always say that the first day, when they put the medicine in, is not the best for results. One needs to wait until the third day, even the fourth. Today, for instance, everything's just about right." This knowing comment, accompanied by an equally knowing look, came from a fattish man. Perhaps his chubbiness is really no more than layers of dirt deposited by the water.

"Would it, d'you think, be good to drink?" asks a high-pitched querulous voice which quavers up from somewhere unidentifiable.

"If you feel a cold coming on, down a mugful just before going to bed. If you do that, you won't need to wake up in the night to go for a pee. It's quite extraordinary. You ought to try it." Again, I cannot tell from which of the steam-wreathed faces this wisdom bubbled out.

Turning my gaze from the baths, I stare down at the duckboards on the bathhouse floor where rows of naked men are sitting and sprawling in ugly disarray. Each adopts the posture that best suits him for scrubbing away at whichsoever portion of his body occupies his attention. Among these variously contorted nudists, two attract my most astonished stare. One, flat on his back, is gawping up at the skylight: the other, flat on his stomach, is peering down the drainhole in the floor. Their utter self-abandonment, the totality of their idleness, is somehow deeply impressive. In another part of the forest, as Shakespeare pleasantly put it, a man with a shaven head squats down with his face to the stone of the wall while a younger, smaller man, also shaven-pated, stands behind him pounding away at his shoulders. They seem to have some kind of master-pupil relationship, and the pupil-type is busy playing the part of an unpaid bath-attendant. There is, of course, a genuine bath-attendant also somewhere on the scene. He is, in fact, not giving anyone a massage but merely tilting heated water out of an oblong pail over the shoulders of a seated patron. He looks as though he must have caught a cold because, despite the fearful hotness of the place, he's wearing a sort of padded sleeveless vest. I notice that, by a crooking of his right big toe, his foot is gripped on a camlet rag.

My glance drifts away to light upon a selfish monster hoarding no less than three wash-pails for himself. Oddly enough, he keeps pressing his neighbor to make use of his soap; perhaps in order to inflict upon that defenseless creature a long and slightly loony flow of talk. I strain my ears to catch the conversation, in truth a monologue. "A gun is an imported thing. Something foreign, not something Japanese. In the good old days it was all a matter of sword against sword. But foreigners are cowards, so they dreamt up something dastardly like guns. They don't come from China, though. Long-range fighting with guns is what you'd expect from one of those Western countries. There weren't any guns in the days of Coxinga who, for all his Chinese name, was descended from the Emperor Seiwa through the Minamoto line. Yoshitsune, the best of the Minamotos, was not killed when they say he was. No, indeed. Instead he fled from Hokkaido to Manchuria, taking with him a Hokkaido man especially good at giving advice. Then Yoshitsune's son, calling himself a Manchurian, attacked the Emperor of China and the Great Ming was flat flummoxed. So what did he do? He sent a messenger to the third Tokugawa Shogun begging for the loan of three thousand soldiers. But the Shogun kept the messenger waiting in Japan for two whole years. I can't remember the messenger's name, but he had some name or other. In the end the Shogun sent him down to Nagasaki where he got mixed up with a prostitute. She then had a son. And that son was Coxinga. Of course, when the messenger at last got home to China, he found that the Emperor of the Ming had been destroyed by traitors. . . ." I can't make head or tail of this amazing rigmarole. It sounds so totally barmy, so crazed a mixture of garbled legends and historical untruths, that my attention again drifts away to focus on a gloomy-looking fellow, maybe twenty-five or twenty-six years old, who appears to be steaming his crotch in the medicated water. He wears a vacant expression and seems to be suffering from a swelling

or something. The very young man of seventeen or eighteen who sits beside him, talking
in an affected manner, is presumably some
houseboy from the neighborhood. Next to
this mincing youth I see an odd-looking back.
Each joint in its spine sticks jaggedly out as
though a knotted bamboo-rod had been
rammed up under the skin from somewhere
down between the buttocks. On either side of
the spine, perfectly aligned, are four black
marks like peg-holes on a piquet-board. All
eight places are inflamed, some of them
oozing pus.

Though I've tried to describe each thing as
it appeared before my eyes, I now realize that
there's still so much to write about that, with
my limited skill, I can never set down more
than a fraction of the totality. I was quietly
flinching from the consequences of my own
rash undertaking to describe in every detail
the more spectacular features of a bathhouse
when a bald-skulled oldster, maybe seventy
years old and dressed in a light-blue cotton
kimono, suddenly appeared at the entrance.
This hairless apparition bowed reverentially
to his drove of naked monsters and then
addressed them with the greatest fluency.
"Good sirs," he says, "I thank you for your
regular and daily visits to my humble estab-
lishment. Today it is, beyond these friendly
walls, more than a little chilly; so please, I
beg of you, take your time, both within and
without my spotless baths, to warm your-
selves at comfortable leisure. Hey, you there,

you in charge of the baths, make quite sure that the water is kept at precisely the proper temperature."

To which the bath-attendant briefly answers "Right."

"Now there's an amiable fellow," says the cracked historian of the doings of Coxinga, speaking admiringly of the aged proprietor. "To run this kind of business, you have to have his knack for it."

I was so struck by the sudden appearance of this strange old man that I decided to discontinue my overall surveillance of the bathhouse scene while I concentrated upon a more particularized scanning of so rum an individual. As I watched him, the old man, catching sight of a child some four years old who has just finished bathing, extends a mottled hand and, in that wheedling voice with which the old present their false advances to the young, calls out "Come over here, my master." The child, frightened by that trampled pudding of a face which the gaffer bent upon him, promptly began to scream. The old man looked surprised. "Why! you're crying! What's the matter? Frightened of the old man? Well, I never!" His voice showed that he was genuinely astonished but, soon giving up this coaxing as a bad job, he quickly switched his attentions to the child's father. "Hullo, Gen-san! How are you? A bit cold today, eh? And what about that burglar who broke into the big shop round the corner? Must have been a fathead. He cut a square

hole in the wooden side-gate but then, can you
believe it, took off without nicking a thing.
Must have seen a copper or a watchman, I
suppose. But what a waste of effort, eh!"
Still grinning at the idea of the burglar's rash
stupidity, he turns to someone else. "Isn't it
cold, though! Perhaps, being young, you
don't yet feel how it bites." It seems to me
that, unique in his antiquity, he's the only
person in the building who feels the cold at
all.

Having been thus absorbed for several
minutes in studying the old man's antics, I
had virtually forgotten about all the other
monsters, including my own master who was
presumably still wedged in his boiling corner.
I was jerked from my absorption by a sudden
loud shouting in the middle of the room. And
who should be the source of it but Mr. Sneaze
himself. That my master's voice should be
overloud and disagreeably indistinct is nothing new, but I was a little surprised to hear
it raised in this particular place. I guessed in
a flash that his raucous yawping had been
caused by a rush of blood to his noddle in
consequence of his unwisely protracted im-
mersion in water hotted up to cure all ills.
Naturally, no one would object to such a
hullaballoo, however raspingly unpleasant, if
it were brought on by physical distress: but,
as grew obvious soon enough, my beloved
master, far from being geyser-dizzied out of
his normal senses, was in fact being very much
his own true self when he started bawling in

that thickly violent voice. For the cause of the nasty uproar was a childishly idiotic squabble which he had started with some conceited pup, some totally insignificant houseboy.

"Get away from here! Go on, further off! You're splashing water into my pail." His shouting scraped one's eardrums. One's attitude to such outbursts depends, of course, upon one's point of view. One could, for instance, as I had done, conclude he had just gone potty with the heat. Another, perhaps one generous-minded person in ten thousand, might see a parallel with that courageous tongue-lashing which Takayama Hikokuro dared to inflict upon a bandit. For all I know, that may have been precisely how my master saw himself. But since the houseboy clearly does not see himself in the bandit's role, we are unlikely to witness a successful repetition of that historic encounter.

"I was sitting here long before you came and plumped yourself down." The boy's reply, calmly delivered over his shoulder, was not unreasonable. But, since that answer made it clear that the lad was not prepared to budge, it did not please my master. My master, even though his blood was up, must have realized that neither the words nor the style of their delivery could really be picked upon as those of a bandit, but his howling outburst was not in fact occasioned by the boy's propinquity or any splashing of water. The truth was that, for some considerable time, the boy and his equally young companion had been swapping remarks in a pertly unpleasing manner utterly inappropriate to their age. My master had endured their prattle for as long as he could but, more and more exasperated, had finally blown up. Consequently, even though he had been perfectly civilly answered, the real cause of his fury remained unsoothed and he could not bring himself to leave the place without a last explosion of his heart. "Hobbledehoys," he shouted. "Damned young idiots. Splashing your dirty water in other people's pails."

In my own heart of hearts I felt considerable sympathy for my master, because I too had found the boys' behavior actively distasteful. Nevertheless I was bound to regard my master's behavior during the incident as conduct unbecoming in a teacher. The trouble is that he is, by nature, something of a dry old stick. Far too strict and far too rigid. Not only is he as rough and dessicated as a lump of coke, but he's also cinder-hard. I'm told that years ago when Hannibal was crossing the Alps, the advance of his army was impeded by a gigantic rock inconveniently blocking the mountain-path. Hannibal is said to have soused the stone with vinegar and then to have lit a bonfire underneath it. The rock thus softened he sawed it into segments, like someone slicing fish-paste, and so passed all his army safely on its way. A man like my master, on whom no effect whatever is produced by hours of steady boiling in a medicated bath, ought perhaps to be soused with vinegar and then grilled on an open fire. Failing some such treatment, his granitic obstinacy will not be softened though hordes of houseboys niggle away at the igneous rock of his nature for a hundred thousand years.

The objects floating in the bath and lazing about on the bathroom's floor are all monsters, teratoids dehumanized by the husking of their clothes; and, as such, they cannot be judged by normal civilized standards. In their teratical world anyone can do what he likes, anything can happen. A stomach can re-site itself in a pulmonary location; Coxinga can be blood-kin to the Seiwa Minamotos; and that Mr. Tami, much maligned, may well be unreliable. But as soon as those naked objects emerge from their bathhouse into the normal world, they garb themselves in obedience to the requirements of civilization and, once robed, they resume the nature and behavior-patterns of human beings. My master stands on the threshold between two worlds. Standing as he does between the bathroom and the changing-room, he is poised at the verge of his return to worldliness, to the sad mundanities of man, to the suavities of compromise, the specious words and the accommodating practices of his species in society. If, on the verge of returning to that world, he yet maintains so brute an obstinacy, surely his mokelike stubbornness must be a deep-rooted disease; a disease, indeed, so very firmly rooted as to be virtually ineradicable.

In my humble opinion, there is only one cure for his condition; and that would be to get the principal of his school to give him the sack. My master, being unable to adapt himself to any change of circumstances, would, if sacked, undoubtedly end up on the streets; and, if thus turned adrift, would equally certainly die in the gutter. In short, to sack him would be to kill him. My master loves being ill, but he would very much hate to die. He welters in hypochondriacal orgies of self-pity, but lacks the strength of soul seriously to look on death. Consequently, if anyone scares him with the news that some continued illness must lead to his demise, my craven master will immediately be both terrified out of his wits and, as I see it, terrified also into the best of health. Only the terror of death by dismissal can shrivel the roots of his almost ineradicable stubbornness. And if dismissal doesn't do the trick, well then, that, I'm afraid, is that; and the poor old perisher will perish. Still and all, that foolish fond old man, sick or well, remains my master. It was he who in my kittenhood took me in and fed me. I recall the tale of the Chinese poet who, given a meal when starving, later repaid that debt by saving his benefactor's life; and I consider it should not be impossible for a cat at least to be moved by his master's fate.

My soul brims full with pity and I become so preoccupied with the internal spectacle of the generous workings of my own deep-feeling heart that, once again, my attention wandered from the scene sprawled out below me. I was sharply brought back to reality by a hubbub of abuse coming from the medicinal bath. Thinking that maybe another squabble has broken out, I shift my gaze to find the throng of monsters all shoving and shouting as they struggle to get out of the narrow cleft of the adit to the bath. Horribly hairy legs and horrible hairless things are juxtaposed and tangled in a horrible squirm to escape. It is the early evening of an autumn day and a red-gold flattish light burns here and there upon the boiling steam which rises up to the ceiling. Through the hot foggy veils whose swirlings fill the room I catch appalling glimpses of wild stampeding monsters. Their shrieks and bellows pierce my ears, and from all sides their agonized shouting that the bloody water's boiling mix in my skull as one loud howl of anguish. The shouts were multicolored: some yellow with sheer fear, some a despairing blue, some furiously scarlet, some a revengeful black. They spilt across each other, filling the bathroom with crashing columns of indescribable noise, the din of pandemonium, such sounds as have no context but Hell and the public bathhouse. Fascinated by this truly awful sight, I just stood there as though riveted to my ledge. The hideous roar climbed to a sort of blubbering climax where the pressure of mindless sound seemed just about to burst the walls apart when, from the swaying mass of tumbling naked bodies, a veritable giant lifted into view. He stands a good three inches taller than the tallest of his fellows. Not only that, but his radish-colored face is thickly bearded. The effect is so remarkable that one daren't affirm that the beard is actually growing on that face. It might be that the face has somehow got entangled in that beard. This apparition emits a booming sound like a large cracked temple-bell struck in the heat of noon. "Pour in cold water. Quick," he thundered. "This bath is on the boil." Both voice and face towered above the squawking rabble around him, and for a moment a sort of silence reigned. The giant had become the only person in the room. A superman; a living embodiment of Nietzsche's vision of Uebermensch; the Demon King among his swarm of devils; the master-monster; Tyrannosaurus Rex. As I stood goggling at him, someone beyond the bath answered through the sudden calm with a grunting cry of "Yah." Assent? Derision? I shall never know. All I can say is that when I peered through the dark haze to identify the source of that ambiguous response, I could just make out the figure of the bathhouse-attendant, padded still in his sleeveless vest, using all his strength to heave a whacking great lump of coal into the opened lid of the furnace. The coal made cracking sounds, and the attendant's profile came radiantly alight. Behind his body the brick wall gleamed with fire and the reflected glare burned at me through the darkness.

Thoroughly alarmed, I reared back from the window and, with one turning spring, hopped down and ran off home. But as I ran I pondered what I'd seen and the conclusions were clear. Although the human creatures in that bathhouse had been seeking a monstrous equality by stripping off their clothes, even from that leveling stark-nakedness a hero had emerged to tower above his fellows. I did not know what had happened to that hero, but I was certainly sure that equality is unachievable however stark things may become.

On reaching home, I find that all is peaceful. My master, his face still glowing from the bath, is quietly eating supper: but, catching sight of me as I jump up onto the veranda, he breaks his silence to remark "What a happy-go-lucky cat! I wonder what he's been up to, coming home as late as this."

My master has little money, but I note that on the table tonight there are laden dishes for a three-course meal. Grilled fish will be one of them. I don't know what the fish is called, but I guess it was probably caught in the sea off Shinagawa sometime yesterday. I have already expatiated at length upon the natural healthiness of fish as fostered by their salt environment; but once a fish has been caught and boiled or, like this one, grilled, questions of environmental advantage are just no longer relevant. This fish would have done much better to stay alive in the sea, even if, in the course of time, it had eventually to suffer such ills as all fish-flesh is heir to. So thinking, I sat

myself down beside the table. I pretended not
to look while looking; looking, in particular,
for a chance to snatch a piece of anything
edible. Those who do not know how to look
while not looking must give up any hope of
ever eating good fish. My master pecked in
silence at the fish, but soon put down his
chopsticks as if to say that he didn't much
like the taste. His wife, seated directly opposite him in matching silence, is anxiously
watching how his chopsticks move up and
down and whether my master's jaws are
opening and closing.

"I say," he suddenly asked her, "give that
cat a whack on the head."

"What happens if I whack it?"

"Never you mind what happens: just
whack it."

"Like this?" asks his wife, tapping my
head with the palm of her hand. It didn't
hurt at all.

"Well, look at that! It didn't give the least
miaow."

"No," she says, "it didn't."

"Then whack it again."

"It'll be just the same, however often I
try." She gave me another tap on the head.
Since I still felt nothing, I naturally kept
quiet. But what could be the point of these
peculiar orders? As a prudent and intelligent
cat, I find my master's behavior utterly in-
comprehensible. Any person who could
understand what he's driving at, would then
know how to react; but it's not that easy. His

wife is simply told to "whack it," but she the whacker is self-statedly at a loss to know why she should whack; and I, the unfortunate whackee, am no less lost to understand what it's all about. My master is becoming a little edgily impatient, for twice already his instructions have failed to produce the result which he only knows that he desires. It is therefore almost sharply that he says "Whack it so that it miaows."

His wife assumed a resigned sort of expression and wearily asking "Why on earth should you want to make the wretched thing miaow?" gave me another, slightly harder, slap. Now that I know what he wants, it's all absurdly easy. I can satisfy my master with a mere miaow; but it's really rather depressing, not just to witness but actually to participate in, yet another demonstration of his addle-pated conduct. If he wanted me to miaow, he should have said so. His wife would have been spared two or three totally unnecessary efforts, and I would not have needed to endure more than a single whack. An order to whack should only be given when only a whack is wanted, but in this case what was wanted was simply a miaow. Now whacking may indeed fall within his sphere of respon-sibility, but miaowing lies in mine. It's a damned impertinence that he should dare to assume that an instruction to whack includes or implies an instruction to miaow, which is a matter totally within my discretion. If he is taking my miaows for granted, indeed he presumes too far. Such failure to respect another person's personality, a deadly insult to any cat, is the sort of crude insensitivity which one must expect from creatures like my master's own particular pet aversion, the nauseous Mr. Goldfield. But the same behavior on the part of my master, a man so confident of his open-heartedness that he struts about stark-naked, can only be seen as an act of unwonted weakness. Yet, as I know, my master is not mean. From which it follows that his venture into whacking was not motivated by any deviousness or malice. In my opinion, his orders were hatched in a brain as guileless and dim as that of a mosquito-larva. If one gobbles rice, one's stomach becomes full. If one is cut, one bleeds. If one is killed, one dies. Therefore, such reasoning runs, if one is whacked, one must perforce miaow. Though I have done my best to justify my master's ways toward me, I regret to be bound to point out the clottish absurdity of such a style of logic. For if one were to concur in that logic, it would follow that if one falls in a river, one is required to drown; that if one eats fried fish, one must then get the squitters; that if one gets a salary, one must turn up for work; and that if one studies books, one cannot fail to make oneself a great name in the world. If that were the way things worked, there'd be some a bit embarrassed. I, for instance, would find it annoying to be obliged to miaow when whacked. What, I ask, would be the point of being born a cat if, like the bell-clock at Mejiro, one is expected to give off sounds every time one's struck? Having thus mentally reprimanded my presumptuous master, then and then only I obliged him with a mew.

As soon as I miaowed, my master turned to his wife. "Hear that?" he said. "Now tell me, is a miaow an interjection or an adverb?"

The question was so abrupt that Mrs. Sneaze said nothing. To tell the truth, my own immediate reaction was to think that, after all, he really had been driven out of his mind by his experiences in the bathhouse. He is, of course, well-known in the neighborhood for his eccentricities. I've even heard him called a clear case of neurosis. However, my master's self-conceit is so unshakable that he insists that, far from being a neurotic himself, it is his detractors in whom neurotic tendencies are clear. When his neighbors call him a dog, he calls them, in mere fairness, so he puts it, filthy pigs. He seems, indeed, besotted with maintaining his ideas of fairness: to the point of being a positive public nuisance. He really sees nothing odd in asking questions as ludicrous as that last enquiry to his wife about the proper parsing of a cat's miaow; but to the general run of his listeners his questions do suggest a certain mental instability. At all events his wife, understandably mystified, makes no attempt to answer him. For obvious reasons, I too can offer nothing in reply.

My master waited for a moment and then,

His wife looked up in surprise and answered "Yes?"

"Is that 'yes' an interjection or an adverb? Tell me now, which is it?"

"Whichever it is, it surely doesn't matter. What a silly thing to ask!"

"On the contrary, it matters a very great deal. That grammatical problem is an issue currently preoccupying the best brains among leading authorities on linguistics in Japan."

"Gracious me! You mean that our leading authorities are bending their brains to a cat's miaow? What a dreadful state of affairs. Anyway, cats don't speak in Japanese. Surely, a miaow is a word from the language of cats."

"That's precisely the point. The problem is a hard one in the very difficult field of comparative linguistics."

"Is that indeed so?" She is clearly sufficiently intelligent to be disinterested in such silly matters. "And have these leading authorities yet discovered what part of speech compares with a cat's miaow?"

"It's so serious a problem that it can't immediately be resolved." He munches away at that fish, and then proceeds to tuck into the next course of stewed pork and potatoes.

"This will be pork, won't it?"

"Yes, it's pork."

"Huh," he grunted in tones of deep disdain. "Huh," and then guzzled it down. Thereafter, holding out a *saké* cup, "I'll have another cup."

"You're drinking rather a lot today. Already you look quite red."

"Certainly I'm drinking," he began, but broke off to veer away on a new mad tack. "Do you know," he demanded, "the longest word in the world?"

"I think I've heard it somewhere. Let me think now. Yes. Isn't it 'Hoshoji-no-Nyudo-Saki-no-Kampaku-dajodaijin'?"

"No, I don't mean a title like that 'Former Chief Adviser to the Emperor and Prime Minister.' I mean a true long word."

"Do you mean one of those crab-written sideways words from the West?"

"Yes."

"Well then, no. That I wouldn't know. But I do know that you've had quite enough *saké*. You'll have some rice now, won't you? Right?"

"Wrong. First I'll drink some more. Would you like to know that longest word?"

"All right. But after, you'll have some rice?"

"The word is 'Archaiomelesidonophrunicherata.' "

"You made it up."

"Of course I didn't. It's Greek."

"What does it mean in Japanese?"

"I don't know what it means. I only know its spelling. Even if written sparingly it will cover about six and a quarter inches."

It is my master's singularity that he makes this sort of statement, which most men would vouchsafe in their cups, in dead cold sobriety. All the same, it's certainly true that he's drinking far too much tonight. He normally limits himself to no more than a couple of cups of *saké,* and he's already tossed back four. His normal dosage turns his face quite red, so the double dosage has inevitably flushed his features to the color of red-hot tongs. He looks to be in some distress, but he keeps on knocking them back. He extends the cup again. "One more," he says.

His wife, finding this really too much, makes a wry face. "Don't you think you've had enough? You'll only get a pain."

"Never mind the pain. From now on, I'm going to train myself into a steady drinker. Omachi Keigetsu has recommended that I devote myself to drink."

"And who may this Keigetsu be?" Great and famous though he is, in the eyes of Mrs. Sneaze he isn't worth a ha'penny.

"Keigetsu is a literary colleague, a first-rate critic of these present times. He has advised me to spend less time at home communing with a cat, to get out and about and to drink on all occasions. Since he's almost a doctor, albeit one of literature, it would seem all right to drink on doctor's orders."

"Don't be so ridiculous! I don't care what he's called or who he is. It's none of his business to urge other people to drink; especially people who happen to have weak stomachs."

"He didn't just recommend drinking. He also said I ought to be more sociable and take a fling at the fast life: wine, women, song, even travel."

"Are you actually trying to tell me that a so-called first-class critic has been making such outrageous suggestions? What kind of a man can he be? Truly, I'm shocked to learn that presumably responsible literary figures would recommend that a married man should go out on the loose."

"There's nothing wrong with living it up. If I had the money, I wouldn't need Keigetsu's encouragement before giving it a try."

"Well then, I'm very glad that you don't have the money. It would be quite awful if a man your age started gallivanting about with wanton girls and drunken half-wit critics."

"Since the idea seems to shock you, I'll scrap my plans for kicking over the traces. However, in consideration of that connubial self-sacrifice, you'll have to take better care of your husband and, in particular, serve him better dinners."

"I'm already doing the best I can on what you give me."

"Really? Well in that case, I'll postpone my investigation of the fast life until I can afford it; and, for tonight, I won't take any more *saké*." With what might just pass for a smile, he held out his rice-bowl for his wife to fill from the container. As I remember it, he thereupon got through three great bowlfuls of mixed rice and tea.

My meal that night consisted of three slices of pork and the grilled head of that nameless fish.